Theft of Sovereignty

Salvatore Santoro

Theft of Sovereignty

ISBN: 0615464599
ISBN-13: 9780615464596

LCCN:

Dedication

This book is dedicated to my three children Kimberly, Rebecca, Lui and all the youth in America. I am apologizing in advance for the strain our generation has put on your future by our absolute lack of vigilance to protect the liberty and freedom that was given to us by our Founding Fathers. I hope it is not too late for us to turn the tide of despotism for you and your children.

Theft of Sovereignty

Table of Contents

Theft of Sovereignty

Salvatore Santoro

Acknowledgements

I want to thank my partner in this endeavor my wife of thirty years. She is the angel over my shoulder and the conscience in my thoughts. She has spent more time editing and reading my work than I have spent writing it.

Theft of Sovereignty

Introduction

In an effort to expose the last century's entangled web of corruption in American politics I have been plagued with the enormity of the task. To properly document the chronology of events that have lead to where we are today would take volumes the size of Britannica. For the uninitiated I have briefly covered a broad range of topics in some sort of historical order that could be followed. For those of you who are students of American liberty you may find some areas of the book elementary. With the premise that there may be readers that have never read our Constitution and don't know the commerce clause from Santa Claus I have had to explain some things from their origins. The most intriguing part of the work is exposing the associations of the characters. You can't have an exhibit of corruption without cronyism. As the cronies are exposed from chapter to chapter I challenge you to remember where they are mentioned in previous chapters and make the connections. I suggest you look at this work as a primer to lead you into more research of the facts brought to light. But my real passion is that I can put into your heart an enduring fire of liberty and patriotism. I believe America is the greatest nation on earth founded by lovers of freedom. The only way for that freedom to survive is for the citizens of this great country to unite in a fight to bring back the early ideas that conceived this great self governing experiment called the land of the free and the home of the brave.

Chapter I

"The Founding Fathers"

"The Founding Fathers", an expression that should bring pause and reflection to every American that would call themselves a patriot. An ideological phrase that should engender in the American heart hope and inspiration in a world gone mad, a terminology that brings to mind heroes, principled men who were aware of the great human challenges besetting them on every side as we face today. They were gallant persons of discerning wisdom unparalleled in their time who rose up against a tyrannical monarchy. These men were pressed on every side by the authoritarian ideology of British imperialism emanating from the most formidable powers the eighteenth century world had to offer. This righteous struggle produced in their hearts a revolutionary tenacity that would conceive the greatest republic the world has ever known, The United States of America.

With a tiny seed of a Continental Congress, a small militia, without a financial system, finances, or a treasury our Founding Fathers succeeded to bring forth unprecedented victory for the liberty of men. Victory born out of a dissention with the status quo of a superpower controlled by an elite British aristocracy bent on world domination. A determined band of militiamen led by one of America's greatest heroes, George Washington went face to face into the jaws of the strongest military war machine of the eighteenth century and won our freedom. On September 3, 1783 this victory was realized when Benjamin Franklin, John Adams and John Jay signed the Treaty of Paris giving America its independence. With the dawning of this glorious day our Founding Fathers were faced with the immediate challenge of forming a new government that would protect our liberty.

With a judicious apprehension of the deteriorated governments of the past the drafters of this new sovereignty were given a divine opportunity at arranging a credo of governance. For the people and by the people it was to govern. They turned to the pattern that had earlier inspired the revolution as they had written in the Declaration of Independence.

"We hold these truths to be self-evident, that all men are created equal, that they are endowed by their Creator with certain unalienable Rights, that among these are Life, Liberty and the pursuit of Happiness."

The most famous sentence in the English language became the foundation of American government and the essence of our Constitution and Bill of rights, for the express purpose of protecting personal liberty. Abraham Lincoln considered the Declaration to be the foundation of his political philosophy, and promoted the idea that:

"The Declaration of Independence is a statement of principles through which the United States Constitution should be interpreted."

These documents came forth from the same men and they are the collective ideological basis of the whole republic and must be understood as such.

As the Constitution of the United States was being prepared the principle of personal liberties was interlaced with republican literature, the Cato letters, John Locke, Polybius, Montesquieu and common law drawn from the Magna Carta. A system of checks and balances would have to be created to prevent the same tyranny and dictatorships that wreaked havoc in the other nations of the world. It is important to understand that to protect the liberties of the American citizens the Founding Fathers instituted a republic not a democracy. There are distinct and subtle differences between the two; the term democracy loosely translated is the mere popular type of government that uses free elections. The modern term democracy is mistakenly used in everyday vernacular to refer to free governments. The particular difference is that in a democracy the majority has unlimited power and provides no safeguards to protect the rights and liberties of the minority. In contrast, a republic limits the power of the majority by a written constitution to protect the rights of the minority. Democracy in various forms direct or representative is "Rule by omnipotent Majority" all elected officials in the legislative or parliamentary assembly render all decisions on a 51 percent vote. Majority rule can remove liberties from the minority.

Thomas Jefferson had this to say about majority rule;

"All the powers of government, legislative, executive, judiciary, result to the legislative body. The concentrating these in the same hands is precisely the definition of despotic government. It will be no alleviation that these powers will be exercised by a plurality of hands, and not by a single one. 173 despots would surely be as oppressive as one."

James Madison wrote in the Federalist Papers Number 10 and 48 on the topic of "excesses of democracy"

"Theoretic politicians, who have patronized this species of government, have erroneously supposed, that by reducing mankind to a perfect equality in their political rights, they would, at the same time, be perfectly equalized and assimilated in their possessions, their opinions, and their passions."

The emphasis of the Founders system of government was based on the principles of the Declaration of Independence, Constitution and Bill of Rights strictly limiting the powers of the majority against the God-given, unalienable and basic rights of the individual. A republic form of government is actually in direct opposition to a democratic system of unlimited power to a majority. Unlimited power of the majority was found to be repugnant by our Founding Fathers. They believed that government was to be contained inside a box of parameters defined by the liberties of the founding documents.

Madison writes in *The Federalist* (no. 55)

"As there is a degree of depravity in mankind which requires a certain degree of circumspection and distrust: So there are other qualities in human nature, which justify a certain portion of esteem and confidence. **Republican government (that of a Republic) presupposes the existence of these qualities in a higher degree than any other form.** *Were the pictures which have been drawn by the political jealousy of some among us, faithful likenesses of the human character, the inference would be that there is not sufficient virtue among men for self government; and that nothing less than the chains of despotism can*

restrain them from destroying and devouring one another."

Three branches of government were created by the Constitution. The executive branch led by the President, the legislative branch divided by a senate and House of Representatives, and the judicial branch controlled by the Supreme Court. The Constitution became the framework for the organization of the United States government and for the accord of the federal government with the states and citizens within the United States to protect the personal liberty of all. The original Constitution was ratified in congress September 17, 1787;

Although it was ratified in congress, without the ratification by the several states it was void of any power. The states were not convinced this Constitution was able to protect against the confiscations of liberty by despotism. Some believed that the original Articles of Confederation were sufficient; they gave the state governments more authority than the federal government. This gave rise to a split debate between Federalists and anti- Federalists. Federalist like James Madison believed that the National government was too week under the Articles of Confederation and could not operate efficiently. While anti-Federalist like Patrick Henry believed that abuse of power by the congress would be inevitable and the position of the President would evolve into a monarchy taking away the power of the local governments and the voice of the people.

In every state resistance to the Constitution was forceful. This strong dissent was preventing the ratification. The demand for a bill of rights to further limit the power of the federal government was called upon by those in opposition. After long debate

Congress sent a set of twelve amendments to the states. Ten of these amendments were immediately ratified and became known as the Bill of Rights. Thus, while the Anti-Federalists were unsuccessful in their quest to prevent the adoption of the Constitution, their efforts produced the Bill of Rights. The Preamble to the Bill of Rights clearly stated its solemn purpose.

*"The Conventions of a number of the States, having at the time of their adopting the Constitution, expressed a desire, **in order to prevent misconstruction or abuse of its powers, that further declaratory and restrictive clauses should be added:** And as extending the ground of public confidence in the Government, will best ensure the beneficent ends of its institution."*

Obviously the Phrase ***"in order to prevent misconstruction or abuse of its powers,"*** is the motivation for the affirmation in writing of the fears expressed by the Anti-Federalist and reflected in the amendments subsequent addition to the Constitution. They understood from looking at history that in time the people would be in a struggle with the ruling bodies attempting to abuse their powers as we are today. The amendments addressed the basic human liberties of the governed in such a way that would make it possible for the people to have strong mechanisms to win that struggle. As patriotic Americans we should have a detailed understanding of these amendments specifically what they meant to the people who ratified them on December 15, 1791 and what has been done throughout history to usurp their meaning and authority.

Amendment 1

Congress shall make no law respecting an establishment of religion, or prohibiting the free exercise thereof; or abridging the freedom of speech, or of the press, or the right
of the people peaceably to assemble, and to petition the Government for a redress of grievances.

Amendment 2
A well regulated Militia, being necessary to the security of a free State, the right of the people to keep and bear Arms, shall not be infringed.

Amendment 3
No Soldier shall, in time of peace be quartered in any house, without the consent of the Owner, nor in time of war, but in a manner to be prescribed by law.

Amendment 4
The right of the people to be secure in their persons, houses, papers, and effects, against unreasonable searches and seizures, shall not be violated, and no Warrants shall issue, but upon probable cause, supported by Oath or affirmation, and particularly describing the place to be searched, and the persons or things to be seized.

Amendment 5
No person shall be held to answer for a capital, or otherwise infamous crime, unless on a presentment or indictment of a Grand Jury, except in cases arising in the land or naval forces, or in the Militia, when in actual service in time of War or public danger; nor shall any person be subject for the same offence to be twice put in jeopardy of life or limb; nor shall be compelled in any criminal case to be a witness against himself, nor

be deprived of life, liberty, or property, without due process of law; nor shall private property be taken for public use, without just compensation.

Amendment 6
In all criminal prosecutions, the accused shall enjoy the right to a speedy and public trial, by an impartial jury of the State and district wherein the crime shall have been committed, which district shall have been previously ascertained by law, and to be informed of the nature and cause of the accusation; to be confronted with the witnesses against him; to have compulsory process for obtaining witnesses in his favor, and to have the Assistance of Counsel for his defense.

Amendment 7
In suits at common law, where the value in controversy shall exceed twenty dollars, the right of trial by jury shall be preserved, and no fact tried by a jury shall be otherwise reexamined in any Court of the United States, than according to the rules of the common law.

Amendment 8
Excessive bail shall not be required, nor excessive fines imposed, nor cruel and unusual punishments inflicted.

Amendment 9
The enumeration in the Constitution, of certain rights, shall not be construed to deny or disparage others retained by the people.

Amendment 10
The powers not delegated to the United States by the Constitution, nor prohibited by it to the States, are reserved to the States respectively, or to the people.

These are the original ten amendments. There are to date 27 amendments made to our constitution. The thirteenth amendment ratified on January, 31 1865 abolished slavery in the United States. The eighteenth amendment brought prohibition while the twenty first amendment repealed it. The nineteenth amendment gave women the right to vote while the twenty sixth amendment lowered the voting age to 18. The last amendment was ratified on May 7, 1992 and has to do with the compensation for congressional salaries.

The Founding Fathers knew that this newly formed government would be beset with unforeseen challenges that would require perpetual vigilance to the principles they had set forth in the Constitution. They believed it was the right of the governed to monitor those in power. The Declaration of Independence expressed:

"…..That to secure these rights, Governments are instituted among Men, deriving their just powers from the <u>consent of the governed</u>, That whenever any Form of Government becomes destructive of these ends, it is the Right of the People to alter or to abolish it, and to institute new Government, laying its foundation on such principles and organizing its powers in such form, as to them shall seem most likely to effect their Safety and Happiness……"

"Consent of the governed" what every American needs to re-assimilate into their thinking is that it is our government we own it *" a government of the people by the people and for the people."* The Founding Fathers understood that power must be ultimately in the hands of the people for this new government to not stray off the course they intended. The freedom to assemble, the

right to freedom of speech and the press, the right to bear arms were all to insure that the lawful citizens of the United States would never have to fear their own government. The early colonist had an experiential knowledge that the people of America today cannot grasp. They endured the British army moving into their homes and quartering themselves there at will. Could you imagine that happening today?

Even with the Constitution and the Bill of Rights the basic truths set forth by our forefathers have for over two centuries been under attack from outside and inside pressures. A contemplative study of American history reveals that from the very first congress influences have been at work to thwart the advance of liberty that our great nation received as a result of our victory in the American Revolution. Some of the fears that had been expressed by the Anti-Federalists would prove to be accurate.

Economic, military, domestic, international, environmental and religious issues from inside and outside of our government, play a dramatic role in our political theater. The citizens of America have always debated the portion of government to allot to the problems facing our people. The role that national or state governance should take in each issue has become a war of epic proportion and has created political parties. The social debates rage on seemingly to no resolution or superiority from either side. The Framers understood that specific changes to the Constitution could be paramount to its destruction; although they could not foresee the problems that would be faced by the generations that followed they understood that the Constitution in no means perfect would have to be amended. So they provided checks and balances for this to take place with much contemplation and debate making modification and ratification a crucial process.

Because of the difficulty of the checks and balances process there have arisen forces that are opposed to the system of government implemented by our Founding Fathers. These forces lean towards alternate forms of government that bring swifter solutions but at the expense of the liberty of their citizens. Ideas that try to circumvent the checks and balances that were instituted by the framers of the Constitution are tested time and time again by those infiltrating our government through the election process and financial process.

The main problem with all governments is that the leaders are human, subject to all the problems of their human nature. Abuse of power in government is as ancient as the dawn of humanity itself. Government is the authority over its people and those in control have always benefited from that control. All nations in history who rose to great power have also amassed great wealth for their aristocracy and ruling classes. The newly formed United States of America with its new Constitution and Bill of Rights was no exception. As a matter of fact for over two centuries America has brought this economical phenomenon to its zenith. With America's wide expanse of undeveloped land and massive unexplored national resources entrepreneurs were given an unlimited opportunity to foster a colossal industrialism that has tested what the Framers prepared for with the Constitution. This monumental accumulation of wealth by the American corporate machine brought with it an insurmountable tide of special interest groups. These special interest groups would lie to waste every shred of Constitutional liberty to meet there insatiable lust for money and power. Big oil, big tobacco, drug multinationals, the military industrial complex just about every product that is produced in America or abroad for that matter has their special interest groups. These are comprised of think tanks of academic professionals advancing a specific area of knowledge, learning or technology where members cooperate to effect or to produce solutions within their particular field. Of course, the information that is produced is always tilted in the favor of profits for the group. This information is then presented by their spokespersons called lobbyists in the halls of the Legislatures. One story states that the term lobbyist originated at the Willard Hotel in Washington, DC, where it was used by Ulysses S. Grant to describe the political wheelers and dealers who frequented the hotel's lobby to access Grant who was often there to enjoy a cigar and brandy.

With limitless financial resources gained at the expense of the people special interest groups funnel immense amounts of money to the political campaigns of our elected officials to keep them in office. Then these same politicians are supposed to protect the Constitution and the interest of the people of the United States of America. This is conflict of interests. What self promoting politician is going to vote against the special interest groups that are feathering their political career? This is the fundamental flaw that has for so long sent our government in the perpetual downward spiral that we are faced with today. The government that was created by our Founding Fathers in 1776 is not the same government we have today. It has evolved into something that the Framers would not even recognize. Subtle changes made over a long period of time by different parties fed by a host of issues that were never intended to be dealt with on a federal level have slowly eroded the liberties of the American people. If we continue on this course we will be left without any freedoms at all. The great American experiment will be over and will be replaced with a controlled Orwellian society. America has become apathetic to the needs of liberty. Liberty must be vigilantly cultivated by the people. It is our responsibility to make sure that our elected officials are representing and protecting the Constitution. If they are left unchecked they will sell us out to every corporate dollar they could get their hands on, which is exactly what has happened. Now we have to go back and study our history to see where the infractions on liberty were created. Although some of the perpetrators have passed away, the tears in the fabric of liberty have left their mark on our society. These tears must be mended with the thread of patriotism otherwise we will not pass to our children a free America. Youth of America take heed to become educated using the power of the internet. Read and study the Constitution, the Bill of Rights and all the documents left behind by the Founding Fathers for in them you will find life, liberty and the pursuit of happiness.

Chapter 2

"The 10th amendment, American Ideology of self Government"

Ninth Amendment

"The enumeration in the Constitution, of certain rights, shall not be construed to deny or disparage others retained by the people."

Tenth Amendment

"The powers not delegated to the United States by the Constitution, nor prohibited by it to the States, are reserved to the States respectively, or to the people."

A limited federal government is what the Founders envisioned to unite the thirteen sovereign states. The Constitution was an agreement between the federal government and the several states. The states propagated the ideology of self-governance; the absence of the tyranny of central government and overwhelming reliance on local government. The direct opposite of the monarchial system that they felt was absolute and corrupt which became the reason why the Founding Fathers opposed the British Empire, gained independence from it, and formed the Constitution, exceedingly restricting the powers of the new federal government.

The American Patriots instrumental in the development of the original colonies understood all too well what they had escaped in England. As Lord Acton put it "…**Power tends to corrupt, and absolute power corrupts absolutely…**" They felt that the only way to avert the renewal of a bureaucracy that leads to totalitarian rule was to enumerate (limit to a certain number) the powers of the federal government and to leave all other powers in the hands of the states or the people. The Constitution of the United States of America gives the federal government 18 enumerated powers stated below. If the federal government is doing anything that is not stated in these 18 legal powers it is usurping its authority.

The Congress shall have Power To lay and collect Taxes,
Duties, Imposts and Excises, to pay the Debts and provide
For the common Defense and general Welfare of the United
States; but all Duties, Imposts and Excises shall be uniform
Throughout the United States;

To borrow Money on the credit of the United States;

To regulate Commerce with foreign Nations, and among
The several States, and with the Indian Tribes;

To establish an uniform Rule of Naturalization, and uniform
Laws on the subject of Bankruptcies throughout the United States;

To coin Money, regulate the Value thereof, and of foreign
Coin and fix the Standard of Weights and Measures;

To provide for the Punishment of counterfeiting the Securities and current Coin of the United States;

To establish Post Offices and post Roads;

To promote the Progress of Science and useful Arts, by Securing for limited Times to Authors and Inventors the Exclusive Right to their respective Writings and Discoveries;

To constitute Tribunals inferior to the Supreme Court;

To define and punish Piracies and Felonies committed on
The high Seas and Offenses against the Law of Nations; To declare War, grant Letters of Marque and Reprisal, and
Make Rules concerning Captures on Land and Water;

To raise and support Armies, but no Appropriation of Money to that Use shall be for a longer Term than two Years;

To provide and maintain a Navy;

To make Rules for the Government and Regulation of the
Land and naval Forces;

To provide for calling forth the Militia to execute the Laws
of the Union, suppress Insurrections and repel Invasions;

To provide for organizing, arming, and disciplining, the

Militia, and for governing such Part of them as may be employed in the Service of the United States, reserving to
the States respectively, the Appointment of the Officers, and the Authority of training the Militia according to the
discipline prescribed by Congress;

To exercise exclusive Legislation in all Cases whatsoever,
over such District (not exceeding ten Miles square) as may, by Cession of particular States, and the Acceptance
of Congress, become the Seat of the Government of the United States, and to exercise like Authority over all Places
purchased by the Consent of the Legislature of the State in
which the Same shall be, for the Erection of Forts, Magazines, Arsenals, dock-Yards and other needful Buildings;

To make all Laws which shall be necessary and proper for
carrying into Execution the foregoing Powers, and all other
Powers vested by this Constitution in the Government of the United States, or in any Department or Officer thereof.

The ninth and tenth Amendment to the Constitution conveys this ideology of self government. James Madison said in the Federalist 45:

"powers delegated by the proposed Constitution to the federal government are few and defined. Those which are to remain in the State governments are numerous and indefinite".

Both of the great founders, Thomas Jefferson and James Madison were more than straight forward in their understanding of the American government as a compact between the sovereign states. James Madison, at the Virginia ratification convention said,

"Who are parties to the Constitution? People, but not the people as composing one great body, but the people as composing the thirteen sovereignties".

Alexander Hamilton relied on the same view when later arguing, in Federalist No. 84, Hamilton was wary of articulating specific restrictions on federal power, for he felt it was clear that the **default position** of the federal government was an ***absence of power***, and any specific power existed only by grant from the Constitution:

"[A Bill of Rights] would contain various exceptions to powers not granted; and, on this very account, would afford a colorable pretext to claim more than were granted. For why declare that things shall not be done which there is no power to do?"

James Madison, when referring to the power assumed of the states, used the phrase"... *numerous and indefinite."* The absolute genius of this ideology lies in the fact that all unforeseen futuristic disputes of government that the Founding Fathers could not anticipate in their time would be settled in the halls of the state legislative bodies. This would cause law makers in the states to compete against each other for the best solution to challenges facing our people creating a free market government. If a law enacted by a particular state was viewed as beneficial and popular to the citizens of that state other states would follow suit with enacting the same legislation. On the flip side of that, if the law enacted in that state was found to be detrimental to the welfare of its citizens it would only affect a smaller portion of the American people and the law would most likely be repealed or modified to be more effective for that state. This system of experimental legislative policy creation on a local level gave the people of America a fundamental influence and ability to stay closely involved with their government.

A second major benefit of this system is its natural ability to safeguard the people of America against infiltration of special interest or any group of corrupt men to subvert or covertly impose on America a type of socialistic or totalitarian ideology. In a central government that has indefinite powers over all the people the corrupt influence of special interests have but only one government to infiltrate. In a system of sovereign states that pass their own collective laws who give only limited control to a central government special interest are presented with the conundrum of having to infiltrate many state governments at the same time to accomplish their treachery.

Unfortunately America has suffered greatly at the hands of corrupt special interests and powerful financial institutions controlled by an oligarchy of a small segment of society distinguished by royalty, wealth, family ties, corporate, or military control who pass their influence from one generation to the next.

From these parasites, who rely on public servitude to exist, has come, from the very beginning an onslaught of political maneuvering to reinvent and reinterpret what the Founding Fathers worked so hard to achieve. At the central battle of this war is the ninth and tenth amendments, the enumerated powers of the federal government outlined in Article 1, Section 8 of the constitution, and a phrase in that section used by enemies of the Constitution to reinterpret and expand the powers of the federal government and diminish the power that was from the beginning given to the states. This struggle has produced an inroad of control by special interest to destroy the very fabric of American freedom.

One of the first pivotal battles in the war against the tenth amendment and states rights came in the form of the sixteenth amendment.

Sixteenth Amendment

Passed by Congress July 2, 1909. Ratified February 3, 1913.

(Note: Article I, Section 9 of the Constitution was modified by the 16th Amendment.)

"The Congress shall have power to lay and collect taxes on incomes, from whatever source derived, without apportionment among the several States, and without regard to any census or enumeration."

The sixteenth amendment found to be unconstitutional by the Supreme Court in 1895 undermines the Constitution's contingency for "limiting government" the most important aspect for protecting liberty. The principle basis of the Constitution sought to balance the power of the federal government against the states in order to keep both in check. Article I, Section 9 of the Constitution states:

"No capitation, or other direct Tax, shall be laid unless in Proportion to the Census or Enumeration."

This meant that the federal government could collect revenue from the states according to population, but had to leave the methods of collection to the states. The federal government collected taxes by tariffs, excise taxes and consumption taxes, limiting the amount of money it could raise against individuals by its own authority." According to the Constitution individual citizens were not to pay taxes directly to the federal government. The first federal income tax was imposed during the Civil War; and was removed shortly thereafter. All apportioned taxes were to be collected by the state and the state forward revenues to the federal government.

The Supreme Court case ***Pollock v. Farmers' Loan & Trust Company***, 157 U.S. 429 (1895) Charles Pollock was a Massachusetts citizen who owned only ten shares of stock in the Farmers' Loan & Trust Company. He believed that certain taxes levied by the Wilson-Gorman Act, those imposed on income from property were considered direct taxes therefore making them unconstitutional because they were not apportioned. He sued Farmers' Loan & Trust Company to keep it from paying the tax on his behalf. Pollock lost in the lower courts but finally appealed to the United States Supreme Court, which agreed to hear the case. The court ruled in Pollock's favor, stating that certain taxes levied by the Wilson-Gorman Act, those imposed on income from property, were unconstitutional. The Court treated the tax on income from property as a direct tax. Under the provisions of the Constitution of the United States direct taxes were required to be imposed fair and balanced in proportion to states' population. The tax in question had not been apportioned and, therefore, was invalid. As Chief Justice Fuller stated:

> *1. We adhere to the opinion already announced—that, taxes on real estate being indisputably direct taxes, taxes on the rents or income of real estate are equally direct taxes.*

> *2. We are of opinion that taxes on personal property, or on the income of personal property, are likewise direct taxes.*

> *3. The tax imposed by sections 27 to 37, inclusive, of the act of 1894, so far as it falls on the income of real estate, and of personal property, being a direct tax, within the meaning of the constitution, and therefore unconstitutional and void, because not apportioned according to representation, all those sections, constituting one entire scheme of taxation, are necessarily invalid.*

> *The decrees hereinbefore entered in this court will be vacated. The decrees below will be reversed, and the cases remanded, with instructions to grant the relief prayed. [158 U.S. 601, 638]*

Despite the Supreme Court's ruling, Joint Resolution No. 40, introduced by Senator Nelson Aldrich of Rhode Island was passed by a majority in Congress and the 16th Amendment was born. This was a great blow to the tenth amendment. Nelson Aldrich was the Senate majority leader and Finance Committee Chairman and one of the corporate cronies of his day. He was father in-law to John D. Rockefeller Jr., father to Winthrop Aldrich Chairman of Chase National Bank, and creator of the plan along with Paul Warburg to institute the Federal Reserve Act of 1913 later that year. Here we find one of the first tears in the fabric of liberty. This was in opposition to the Constitution and the Founding Fathers idea of checks and balances to keep the federal government to function without infringing on the rights of free Americans. The 16th Amendment gave the federal government the power to directly tax the individual citizen. Incomprehensible is the absolute power of the press at the time to create the illusion that America would be better served by a direct tax on individuals imposed by the federal government than fundamental Constitutional considerations. This gave the federal government a new power they were never meant to have and the creation of the most complicated bureaucracy known to man, The Internal Revenue Service. Because of this new power the federal government had to produce new funds (garnished from the tax payer) for the creation of federal departments that would usurp matters that previously belonged to the state.

The second pivotal battle in the war on the rights of the states came in the form of the seventeenth amendment. The Constitution clearly defined that the senate was to be composed of individuals appointed by the state legislators. The Constitution states in Article 1, Section 3.

The Senate of the United States shall be composed of two Senators from each State, [chosen by the Legislature thereof,]* for six Years; and each Senator shall have one Vote. Immediately after they shall be assembled in Consequence of the first Election, they shall be divided as equally as may be into three Classes. The Seats of the Senators of the first Class shall be vacated at the Expiration of the second Year, of the second Class at the Expiration of the fourth Year, and of the third Class at the Expiration of the sixth Year, so that one third may be chosen every second Year; [and if Vacancies happen by Resignation, or otherwise, during the Recess of the Legislature of any State, the Executive thereof may make temporary Appointments until the next Meeting of the Legislature, which shall then fill such Vacancies.]

In an effort to make the several states active participants in the federal government and to foster an environment of cooperation the Founders created the senate to act as an overseer and check of the House of Representatives. James Madison also believed that the States should be active participants in the Federal Government when he said,

"Whenever power may be necessary for the national government, a certain portion must be necessarily left with the states, it is impossible for one power to pervade the extreme parts of the United States so as to carry equal justice to them. The state legislatures also ought to have some means of defending themselves against the encroachments of the national government.

In every other department we have studiously endeavored to provide for its self-defense. Shall we leave the states alone un-provided with the means for this purpose? And what better means can be provided than by giving them some share in, or rather make them a constituent part of, the national government?"

The seventeenth amendment ignored the Constitutional provision for the selection of the Senate by the state legislature and modified the election process of the Senate by the national election process. Tear number two in the fabric of liberty. At first glance it seems to be a harmless reform because it allows the people to select Senators by the voting process but this was another attempt by the oligarchy to chip away at the rights of the state.

Prior to the seventeenth amendment U.S. Senators discussed federal affairs with their state legislators on a regular basis. They were given their authority from the state legislators and were constrained by the interest of the local municipalities. If they voted in opposition to the interest of their state they would be removed from their office by the state. The selection of the US senator was not based on expensive campaigns and contributions from special interests. U.S. Senators did not have to raise millions of dollars to run for office. The Founding Fathers new that there would be with only two U.S. Senators per state a difficulty for personally discussing federal affairs with the large number of constituents from each state. The only choice was to have them discuss our federal affairs with the State Legislatures and beholden the US Senators to the state legislatures. Included in the U.S. Constitution, the people of the states enjoyed the right to vote for their U.S. Representatives. The change facilitated the buying of US Senators by the corporations, banks, special interests and other lobbying factors and influences. US Senators no longer answer to their state legislatures or the people nor are they likely to discuss federal matters with them, they are now obligated to their campaign contributors and will most likely be found in the halls and boardrooms of corporate institutions.

Seventeenth Amendment

Passed by Congress May 13, 1912. Ratified April 8, 1913.

(Note: Article I, Section 3 of the Constitution was modified by the 17th Amendment.)

"The Senate of the United States shall be composed of two Senators from each State, elected by the people thereof, for six years; and each Senator shall have one vote. The electors in each State shall have the qualifications requisite for electors of the most numerous branch of the State legislatures. When vacancies happen in the representation of any State in the Senate, the executive authority of such State shall issue writs of election to fill such vacancies: Provided, That the legislature of any State may empower the executive thereof to make temporary appointments until the people fill the vacancies by election as the legislature may direct. This amendment shall not be so construed as to affect the election or term of any Senator chosen before it becomes valid as part of the Constitution."

A third attack on states' rights comes in the form of the Supreme Court decisions expanding the use of one of the federal government's enumerated powers the "commerce clause". This action caused government interference into affairs that the federal government had no jurisdiction to control; this has become not only a tear in the fabric of liberty but a large gaping hole. Article 1, Section 8 of the Constitution states,

"To regulate Commerce with foreign Nations, and among the several States, and with the Indian Tribes;"

Carter v. Carter Coal Company, 298 U.S. 238 (1936 James W. Carter was a shareholder of the Carter Coal Company and opposed the company joining a government program. Carter sued the coal mine claiming that coal mining was not interstate commerce and therefore could not be regulated by the federal government. The question was could the federal government use the clause in Article 1, section 8 in the constitution to regulate production of an industrial commodity like coal. The Supreme Court decided in favor of James W. Carter that coal mining was not considered commerce with the majority opinions as follow:

a) Just because a commodity is manufactured or produced within a state and is intended for interstate commerce, does not mean that its "production or manufacturing is subject to federal regulation under the commerce clause."

b) A commodity that is meant to be sold in interstate commerce is not considered to be part of interstate commerce "before the commencement of its movement from the state."

c) "Mining is not interstate commerce." It is a local business and is subject to local control and taxation.

d) "The word 'commerce' is equivalent to the phrase 'intercourse for the purposes of trade'": the process of mining coal does not fit within this definition.

e) The labor board has powers over production, not commerce. This confirms the idea that production is a purely local activity.

f) If the production of coal by a single person does not have a direct effect on interstate commerce, then the production of coal by many people can also not have a direct effect on interstate commerce.

g) The evils that Congress sought to control are "all local evils over which the federal government has no legislative control."

h) "The federal regulatory power ceases when interstate commerce ends; and, the power does not attach until interstate commercial intercourse begins."

This decision was a devastating blow to president FDR whose new deal policies were entrenched with ideology of government regulation into labor and industry for the purpose of controlling the economy after the great depression. Because of this, Roosevelt tried to appoint additional judges to the Supreme Court. Roosevelt claimed that this was not to change the rulings of the Court but to lessen the load on the older justices. It became known as the FDR court packing plan but widespread opposition killed the deal but FDR kept at it until he tore the veil.

Three years later the "commerce clause" appeared again in front of the Supreme Court in **National Labor Relations Board v. Jones & Laughlin Steel Corporation.** The Jones and Laughlin steel company fired ten employees who wanted to join a labor union. The NLRB opposed the firing of the employees and ordered the steel company to rehire the employees and give them their back pay. The steel company refused citing that the National Labor Relations Act of 1935 was unconstitutional because the steel production was not commerce and therefore could not be regulated by the federal government. The federal law usurped the states mandates and limited the means with which employers may react to workers in the private sector who create labor unions, engage in collective bargaining, and take part in strikes and other forms of concerted activity in support of their demands.

Because of the Supreme Court precedent **Carter v. Carter Coal Company**, lower courts agreed with Jones & Laughlin. But when it got to the Supreme Court FDR had his cronies ready and in what became known as "the switch in time that saved nine", Justice Owen Josephus Roberts and Chief Justice Charles Evans Hughes switched sides in the commerce debate and upheld the National Labor Relations Act, which gave the National Labor Relations Board extensive power over labor relations across the United States. This was a great usurp of state power and exactly what our Founding Fathers feared and found to be repugnant "federal regulation of free market activities". This led to many decisions of the Supreme Court to expand the meaning of the word commerce in the constitution giving the federal government the power to regulate just about everything. Use of the "commerce clause" has spiraled out of control; it has driven passed any rationale the Founders could possibly have intended for this very basic rule. The Supreme Court has created infinite flexibility of the "commerce clause" and as it is presently interpreted allows the federal government to use the Constitution to destroy the freedoms in the document itself. If the Founding Fathers would have been here today to see what happened to the commerce rule and the way the federal government has used it to regulate everything I am sure that they would go back and limit its expansion.

With the passing of the sixteenth and seventeenth amendment and the expanded use of the commerce clause the federal government has taken most power away from the state. The people at the local level that the state represents are opposed by special interests that use the federal governments expanded power to their own ends without the checks and balances that were instituted by our Founding Fathers. A return to basic principles of the Founding Fathers can only be obtained in a campaign to reinstate the principles of sovereignty under the Constitution and the tenth Amendment. Between 2009 and 2010 thirty eight states are already preparing resolutions to accomplish this very thing and nine states have passed resolutions. These statements are demanding that the federal government stop assuming powers that were not given to it by the Constitution and stop regulating and imposing their mandates on the states and their people.

Chapter 3

"Social Theory – Am I a Slave?"

In the ancient systems you had those who conquered and those who were conquered. One tribe or nation conquered another and those who were victorious became the rulers while those who were defeated became the slaves. This system was prevalent from the beginning of society through to the fall of the Roman Empire. In what became known as the dark ages a new form of class struggle emerged into those who possessed land and those who did not possess land creating the lord and serf version of freeman and slave. In the wake of the renaissance arose another form of class distinction due to the new skills that were invented by the guilds for construction, the relation of master and journeyman. Society has always been naturally separated by different classifications of people according to their economic, educational and inheritance status as well as particular religious beliefs. To better understand the dark forces at work in our government a definition of the basic social philosophies of the world have to be explained.

The classes in a society are separated by **means of production** (everything needed to create wealth except human labor) the means of production in an agricultural society included land, tools, raw materials, wells, wagons and storehouses while the means of production in a modern society include factories, machines, infrastructure, mines and natural resources it also includes the distribution of the means such as banks, stores and shipping. Those who owned the "means of production" are separated from those who labor to produce. Governments are formed on the distribution of these two elements.

In **capitalism** the means of production are owned by private interests for the profit of their owners. Prices are controlled by supply and demand, people are free to invest in business or work for the business for a wage or salary therefore defining social classes by accumulated income or wealth and at the very simplest terms breaks them into upper, middle and lower class although there are many other distinctions further breaking down those brackets, for example blue collar or white collar, above or below the poverty level or rich verses wealthy.

The **communist perspective** places the majority of people into only two classes, the proletariat (working class) which includes anyone who makes their living by selling their labor for a wage and the bourgeoisie (ruling class - owners of the means of production) who make their living on the percentage of surplus created by the exploitation of the working class. In an effort to abolish the class system Karl Marx and Friedrich Engles produced the Communist Manifesto a short document that outlined their political ideological process that would produce a classless utopian society. The method to reach this utopian plan demands complete economic equality and produces this by forced income redistribution. The document explains that the ruling class cannot exist without the working class for it is the working class that provides the labor to create the financial surplus that enriches the ruling class therefore by creating organized union resistance and riots if necessary the working class can reduce or eliminate the surplus overthrowing capitalism and giving the proletariat control of the state. Communism also known as belonging to the peoples claims to give all the means of production to the people.

The **socialist perspective** is another attempt to abolish the corruption of capitalism and also maintains the same class struggle argument of the communists only it calls for the nationalization and control by the state of the methods of production and labor. It also advocates state control of capital within the structure of a market economy. Socialism like communism also has a social end of complete equality and through government programs seeks to redistribute wealth.

The **fascist perspective** is a combination of capitalism, communism and socialism and can be considered far right or far left. It will mainly through corporatism gain control of all the means of production and hand them over to the state to control and usually through a strict powerful military presence control the working class in an Orwellian manner.

The least intrusive to the liberties of men of these systems is by far the laissez-faire capitalistic system as long as those who amass the greatest amount of wealth do not use it to control or oppress those in a subordinate position. The long history of abuses of monetary power from ancient Egypt to the twentieth century have given rise to alternate economic systems like communism and socialism that seek to level the playing field. There is no perfect economic system or government because these systems are created by intelligent but imperfect men, usually in response to temporary failures of systems at the time.

Marx's basic principles and theories involved the ruling aristocracy and the workers and totally failed to identify the largest portion of the population, the middle class. Marx incorrectly classified them with the aristocracy. His class warfare philosophy was buffered by the middle class and the struggle by means of labor never made it to the Aristocracy stopping any momentum for natural revolution. Communism never rose to power as Marx theorized but only by the violent military overthrow of oppressive regimes and murder of the ruling class. The attempt by Marx to create equality among all people failed to take into consideration human individuality. Independence and free will can never be suppressed and countless millions of people were slaughtered by the communist regimes in an attempt to unify their state. In the USSR under Lenin the number lies between 20 and 50 million. In Cambodia it is estimated that Pol Pot murdered a fourth of the population for having opposing views. Estimates in China are as high as 45 million.

One of the problems the working class in a communist economic system experiences is the absence of a means to advance his class status. If he works hard and saves his money he can't use it to invest in means of production that can make him move from being a worker to an owner. With no room for advancement the drive to excel is removed diminishing technical advancements in society. The communist system binds the citizen to a single class creating an impenetrable ceiling to advancement.

The similarities between communism and socialism are evident first in their leadership both socialism and communism framed in opposition to the natural human condition of free will require strict enforcement. The administrative complex of these systems form yet another class split, those who enforce and those who are enforced upon. Second, in their ends both have the utopian goal of complete equality in their state. Thirdly, in their means both systems are deeply rooted in their centralized control of financial systems and income redistribution as their primary course to reaching equality.

In stark contrast to communism and socialism is laissez-faire capitalism. The word laissez-faire is the French word for "let do" or "allow happening" and represents a condition in which financial transactions between private individuals are **free** from all government interference. This system is controlled by the consumer in a free market where price is dictated by supply and demand and people are free to use their labor and resources to command their own place among society by entrepreneurship. The largest segment of the middle class in America today is comprised of the small business owner. The greatest era of laissez-faire capitalism in America was from the closing of the Second Bank of the United States by Andrew Jackson to the creation in 1913 of the Federal Reserve. This was the longest period of unregulated economic policy by the US Government spawning the American industrial revolution. Since then modern day capitalism has been slowly diluted by government intervention through controlling finance and banking, regulating the production of natural resources, regulating sales of stock, legislate the power of workers to form unions, set rules for wages and hours, provide unemployment benefits and social security, creating farm subsidies and insuring bank deposits.

The adversities faced by society like unemployment, elderly care, agricultural production, financial downturns and fairness in the workplace are all important issues, they are not in opposition to free market capitalism and the enthusiasm to remedy the adversities faced by society cannot be used to change the system of government handed to us by the Founding Fathers. The politicians of the day have used every social issue of the twentieth century as an impetus for more regulation, more government intervention and more nationalization. Proposed legislation for healthcare reform, TARP Bailouts, stimulus packages, omnibus packages and illegal alien amnesty etc, is causing America to transform towards a fascist state. The government is reaching into all aspects of American daily life more than at any time in our history. Small business is being squeezed out of existence by government regulation that is reducing profit margins. The middle class is the heart of America the current Washington policies will see to eliminating it. If the middle class is eliminated the only thing left will be working for the corporate state. The shackles of government are awaiting those who take their liberties for granted.

With enough Government control we will stop being a constitutional republic and turn into some form of democratic socialist nation like those of the European Union or just some form of fascist capitalism.

Winston Churchill aptly described socialism as *"a philosophy of failure, the creed of ignorance, and the gospel of envy, its inherent virtue is the equal sharing of misery."*

As economist Thomas Sowell put it, *"Socialism in general has a record of failure so blatant that only an intellectual could ignore or evade it."*

Herbert Spencer : *"All socialism involves slavery. That which fundamentally distinguishes the slave is that he labors under coercion to satisfy another's desires."*

Lord Acton *"Socialism means slavery."*

"But how is this legal plunder to be identified? Quite simply. See if the law takes from some persons what belongs to them, and gives it to other persons to whom it does not belong. See if the law benefits one citizen at the expense of another by doing what the citizen himself cannot do without committing a crime.

Then abolish this law without delay, for it is not only an evil itself, but also it is a fertile source for further evils because it invites reprisals. If such a law — which may be an isolated case — is not abolished immediately, it will spread, multiply, and develop into a system.

The person who profits from this law will complain bitterly, defending his acquired rights. *He will claim that the state is obligated to protect and encourage his particular industry; that this procedure enriches the state because the protected industry is thus able to spend more and to pay higher wages to the poor workingmen.*

Do not listen to this sophistry by vested interests. The acceptance of these arguments will build legal plunder into a whole system. In fact, this has already occurred. The present-day delusion is an attempt to enrich

everyone at the expense of everyone else; to make
plunder universal under the pretense of organizing it. "

Frédéric Bastiat
The Law (June 1850)
French economist, statesman, and author

Chapter 4

"Rise of the Great American War Machine"

The United States of America is the greatest client to American and International corporations. All corporations want the government contracts for their respective goods and services and the government buys a lot of goods and services. Also the laws enacted by congress have an economic effect on the sale of goods and services to the public. Corporations use special interests groups to collect and produce information. Then the lobbyists who work for the special interests groups share this information with legislators while contributing to their political campaigns ensuring that the interests of the corporations are effectively brought to bear in Congress to further their quest for market domination.

One of the greatest of all perpetrators of this absurdity is the great American war machine. Corporations have infiltrated so deeply into the American political structure that they have been able to influence our leaders into using the military for monetary gain. In his farewell address to the nation on January 17, 1961 President Dwight D Eisenhower warned of the corporate takeover of the military by unwarranted influence.

"...This conjunction of an immense military establishment and a large arms industry is new in the American experience. The total influence — economic, political, even spiritual — is felt in every city, every statehouse, every office of the federal government. We

*recognize the imperative need for this development. Yet we must not fail to comprehend its grave implications. Our toil, resources and livelihood are all involved; so is the very structure of our society. In the councils of government, **we must guard against the acquisition of unwarranted influence, whether sought or unsought, by the military-industrial complex. The potential for the disastrous rise of misplaced power exists and will persist. We must never let the weight of this combination <u>endanger our liberties or democratic processes</u>. We should take nothing for granted....***"*

This warning by President Dwight D. Eisenhower calls the influence new in the American experience unfortunately this was not the case the influence was there from many years before. Just to begin to shed some light on the subject we turn to one of the military's finest, Major General Smedly Butler.

He joined the Marine Corps in 1898 when the Spanish American War broke out. He earned the Brevet Medal during the Boxer Rebellion in China. He saw action in Central America and in France. During World War I he was promoted to Major General. The most decorated marine in military history after a lifelong service to his country had this to say about the military establishment in a speech delivered in 1933 twenty seven years before President Eisenhower's speech.

"War is just a racket. A racket is best described, I believe, as something that is not what it seems to the majority of people. Only a small inside group knows what it is about. It is conducted for the benefit of the very few at the expense of the masses.

I believe in adequate defense at the coastline and nothing else. If a nation comes over here to fight, then we'll fight. The trouble with America is that when the dollar only earns 6 percent over here, then it gets restless and goes overseas to get 100 percent. Then the flag follows the dollar and the soldiers follow the flag.

I wouldn't go to war again as I have done to protect some lousy investment of the bankers. There are only two things we should fight for. One is the defense of our homes and the other is the Bill of Rights. War for any other reason is simply a racket.

There isn't a trick in the racketeering bag that the military gang is blind to. It has its "finger men" to point out enemies, its "muscle men" to destroy enemies, its "brain men" to plan war preparations, and a "Big Boss" Super-Nationalistic-Capitalism.

It may seem odd for me, a military man to adopt such a comparison. Truthfulness compels me to.

*I **spent thirty- three years and four months in active military service as a member of this country's most agile military force, the Marine Corps. I served in all commissioned ranks from Second Lieutenant to Major-General. And during that period, I spent most of my time being a high class muscle- man for Big***

Business, for Wall Street and for the Bankers. In short, I was a racketeer, a gangster for capitalism.

I suspected I was just part of a racket at the time. Now I am sure of it. Like all the members of the military profession, I never had a thought of my own until I left the service. My mental faculties remained in suspended animation while I obeyed the orders of higher-ups. This is typical with everyone in the military service.

I helped make Mexico, especially Tampico, safe for American oil interests in 1914. I helped make Haiti and Cuba a decent place for the National City Bank boys to collect revenues in. I helped in the raping of half a dozen Central American republics for the benefits of Wall Street. The record of racketeering is long. I helped purify Nicaragua for the international banking house of Brown Brothers in 1909-1912. I brought light to the Dominican Republic for American sugar interests in 1916. In China I helped to see to it that Standard Oil went its way unmolested.

During those years, I had, as the boys in the back room would say, a swell racket. Looking back on it, I feel that I could have given Al Capone a few hints. The best he could do was to operate his racket in three districts. I operated on three continents."

Major General Smedely Butler
United States Marine Core

　　　Seventy seven years have passed since he gave us this warning and not a single thing has changed except the magnitude of the operations. He made a powerfully clear statement of his position after a lifetime of military combat and conquests around the globe describing the only righteous reasons for war. One is to protect our homes and the other is to protect the Bill of Rights. Major Smedley Butler was a true American Patriot that I am sure would have received true honor amongst our Founding Fathers. He lifted the curtain to show us what was really happening during his tenure behind the scenes in the halls of congress by the lobbyists and our leaders. The sad thing about it is that what he said fell on deaf ears and very few people in America today even know he existed.

He mentioned in his speech how he helped make Tampico safe for American oil interests in 1914. Tampico is the main city in the Mexican state of Tamaulipas. It is the nation's chief economic powerhouse on the Gulf of Mexico. It shares its border with the state of Texas. With the arrival in 1910 of Standard Oil, Royal Dutch Shell, Sinclair Oil and Texas Oil to the region the national output of crude oil quickly rose to 12,000,000 barrels making Mexico one of the largest exporters of oil in the world. Francisco I. Madero was at the time President of Mexico. Madero imposed an export tax on all oil production out of Mexico.

BRYAN DEMANDS CUT IN TAMPICO OIL TAX

Constitutionalists Told That Export Duty of Eight Cents a Barrel Is Unreasonable.

BRITISH AND DUTCH PROTEST

Admiral Mayo Reports That No Involuntary Loans Have Yet Been Taken from Foreigners.

Special to The New York Times.

Salvatore Santoro

Transactions of the American Institute of Mining, Metallurgical..., Volume 65 Section 546 by American Institute of Mining Engineers, American Institute of Mining, Metallurgical, and Petroleum Engineers, Metallurgical Society of AIME, Society of Mining Engineers

"...during the administration of President Madero an export tax of 20 centavos per metric ton approximately 1.64 US cents per barrel of oil exported was charged this tax which was applied irrespective of the quality of the oil was in force until November 1913...."

Early in 1913 Madero was overthrown by a coup that involved his general Victoriano Huerta with the help of American Ambassador Wilson Lane. Huerta took control of the Mexican Government and made the fatal mistake of raising the export tax to 8 US cents per barrel of oil. An article in the New York Times stated that then Secretary of State William Jennings Bryan demanded an immediate cut of the export tax. President Woodrow Wilson sent his friend the journalist William Bayard Hale, to Mexico in June 1913 to get firsthand information. Hale was unenthusiastic about Huerta, describing him as "an ape-like old man" who "may almost be said to subsist on alcohol." With Hale's views in mind, President Wilson continued to shun Huerta's government, even though Ambassador Wilson Lane virtually insisted that Huerta be recognized. Acting on the President's orders, Bryan recalled Lane and accepted his resignation.

On April, 9 1914, Mexican authorities mistakenly arrested eight U.S. sailors at Tampico. Huerta's commanding general in the port released the men and apologized to Rear Admiral Henry T. Mayo, the commander of the U.S. squadron at Tampico. Mayo gave Huerta twenty-four hours to make a more formal apology, punish the arresting officer, and fire a twenty-one-gun salute. Using this incident President Woodrow Wilson ordered an increase in U.S. forces in Mexican waters. Congress gave him permission to take punitive action against Mexico on behalf of constitutionality and democracy. Almost Immediately Wilson was alerted to a German delivery of weapons for Victoriano Huerta due to arrive to the port on April 21. As a result, Wilson issued an immediate order to seize the port's customs office and confiscate the weaponry. It was later found out that the shipment of weapons originated from the Remington Arms company in the United States. The vessel Ypiranga was operated by the Hamburg-America Line held by American and German financial interests and ran cargo from New York to Hamburg on regularly scheduled voyages. The landing invasion of Vera Cruz led by Major Smedley Butler had By April 26 5,800 Marines and sailors which held the city for six months because of the tax on oil. By the end of the conflict, the Americans reported 17 dead and 63 wounded and the Mexican forces had 126 dead and 195 wounded. Huerta was forced to resign as President and the export tax on oil was reduced. The most relevant thing was that the security of the oil fields in Mexico after this grand show of muscle, put control firmly in the hand of the international oil Cartel.

Another incident that Major General Smedely Butler refers to is the National City Bank Boys and the occupation of Haiti in 1915. In an effort to limit German influence, in 1910-11 the US State Department backed a consortium of American investors, assembled by the National City Bank of New York (Citibank today), in acquiring control of the *Banque National d'Haïti*, the nation's only commercial bank and the government treasury.

Annals of the American Academy of Political and Social Science, Volumes 99-100 *By American Academy of Political and Social Science, National American Woman Suffrage Association Collection (Library of Congress)*

"...The reorganization was affected in 1910 under the title Banque Nationale de la Republique d'Haiti, and the bank remained a French concern, the Germans having to be satisfied with the allotment of about 2,500 shares to the Disconto Gesellschaft out of a total of 40,000 shares. Some 6,000 shares were held in New York by three firms of close German affiliations. At the outbreak of the War the Germans on the Board of Directors resigned and their interests were taken over by the National City Bank, which had purchased some 2,000 shares about 1911.

Shortly thereafter the French arranged with the National City Bank for the taking over of the management. In February, 1920, arrangements were made to buy the French stock and to apply for a new charter to be granted to the National City Bank."

After this arrangement the country of Haiti was now under the control of the National City Bank in New York (commonly known as the Rockefeller Bank). Who were the National City Bank Boys Major General Butler was talking about? An investigation of the Committee on banking and currency in 1912 led by US House of Representative Arsene J. Pujo, Louisiana found that The National City Bank had 87 directors who were also directors of 47 of the most influential corporations in America controlling oil, railroads, banks, steel companies, utilities and commodity production. Some of the most famous National City Bank boys were William Rockefeller and his older brother John D. Rockefeller whose partnership of Rockefeller & Andrews merged. In 1870, that company became Standard Oil. William Rockefeller served as the company's New York representative until 1911 when Standard Oil of New Jersey was split up by the United States Supreme Court. He also had interests in copper, railways, and public utilities, and built up the National City Bank of New York. Others included James Stillman, President, considered to have been one of the 100 wealthiest Americans. His oldest son, James A. Stillman, also served as president of National City Bank of New York. Stillman was related to even greater wealth by marriage: his two daughters, Sarah Elizabeth Stillman and Isabel Goodrich Stillman, married the sons of his business associate and friend William Rockefeller. E.H. Harriman, director and President of the Union Pacific and Southern Pacific Railroads. Jacob Henry Schiff, the director of many important corporations, including the National City Bank of New York, Equitable Life Assurance Society, Wells Fargo & Company, and the Union Pacific Railroad. Henry Clay Frick, Founder of the H. C. Frick & Company coke manufacturing company, was chairman of the Carnegie Steel Company, and played a major role in the formation of the giant U.S. Steel manufacturing concern. He also financed the construction of the Pennsylvania Railroad and the Reading Company, and owned extensive real estate holding in Pittsburgh and throughout the state of Pennsylvania. J. P. Morgan Jr., Son of John Pierpont

Morgan who was an American financier who dominated corporate finance. In 1892 Morgan arranged the merger of Edison General Electric and Thomson-Houston Electric Company to form General Electric. After financing the creation of the Federal Steel Company he merged in 1901 the Carnegie Steel Company and several other steel and iron businesses, including Consolidates Steel and Wire Company owned by William Edenborn, to form the United States Steel Corporation. Jonathon Ogden Armour, an American meatpacking magnate in Chicago, and owner and president of Armour and Company. During his tenure as president, Armour & Co. expanded nationwide and overseas, growing from a small regional meatpacker to one of the largest food products companies in the United States. Cyrus McCormack, Founder of International Harvester and Joseph Peter Grace, son of William Russell Grace Mayor of New York and Founder of the W. R. Grace and Company Chemical Giant were also on the board.

"...The table further shows that National City Bank of New York has 32 directorships in 16 banks and trust companies, namely: Central Trust Company Chicago 1, Continental and Commercial National Bank, Chicago 3, Continental and Commercial Trust and Savings Bank, Chicago 1, Merchants Loan and Trust Company, Chicago 1, Mellon National Bank, Pittsburgh 1, Union Trust Company,

National City Bank of NY
Pittsburgh 1, American Security and Trust Company, Washington 1, Riggs National Bank, Washington 1, Bank of

Theft of Sovereignty

Manhattan Company, New York 1, Central Trust Company, New York 1, Farmers Loan and Trust Company, New York 9, Guaranty Trust Company, New York 1, Hanover National Bank, New York 1, National Bank of Commerce, New York 3, New York Trust Company, New York 3, United States Trust Company, New York 3 Having total resources of $1,532,000,000 and total deposits of $1,130,000,000.

One director in 1 insurance company, namely, Mutual Life Insurance Company of New York, having total assets of $587,000,000.

28 Directorships in 17 Railroad Companies, namely, Atchinson, Topeka & Santa Fe 1, Baltimore & Ohio 1, Chesapeake & Ohio 1, Chicago, Milwaukee & Saint Paul 3, Chicago & Northwestern 3, Delaware, Lackawanna & Western 5, Illinois Central 1, Missouri, Kansas & Texas 1, New York Central & Hudson River 2, New York, New Haven & Hartford 1, Norfolk & Western 1, Northern Pacific 1, Pennsylvania 1, Reading Co 1, Seaboard Airline 1, Southern Pacific 2, Union Pacific 2, having a total capitalization of $8,308,000,000 and a total mileage of 100,400.

One Director in 1 steamship company, namely, International Mercantile Marine, having a total capitalization of $173,000,000 and total gross annual earnings of $39,000,000

Fifteen Directorships in 9 producing and trading companies, namely: Amalgamated Copper Co 1, American Sugar Refining Company 2, Armour and Co 2, Baldwin Locomotive Works 1, Central Leather Company 1, Inter-Continental Rubber Co 1, International Harvester 1, Lackawanna Steel 4, United States Steel Corp 2, having a total capitalization of $2,211,000,000 and total gross annual earnings in excess of $812,000,000.

Nine Directors in 3 public utility companies, namely: Chicago Elevated Railways 2, Consolidated Gas Co 6, New York Railway Co 1, having a total capitalization of $394,000,000 and total annual gross earnings of $72,000,000.

In all 86 Directors in 47 corporations with total capitalization of $13,205,000,000."

Investigative Subcommittee of the Committee on banking and currency US House of Representatives Arsene J. Pujo, Louisiana, Chairman. Excerpt from exhibit 134-c December 18, 1912 explanation *of table of interlocking directorates*

Now that we know who the National City boys were the story in Haiti goes like this:

Jean Vilbrun Guillaume Sam the Haitian Dictator at the time was being opposed by anti American Rosalvo Bobo. American business interests in Haiti such as the Haitian American Sugar Co. and the Banque Nationale de la Republique d'Haiti owned by National City were now in danger of financial loss. To preserve American corporate dominance over Haiti's banking and sugar lands the National City boys influenced President Woodrow Wilson to send 330 U.S. Marines to Port-au-Prince on July 28, 1915 among them were Smedley Butler, Ross Lams and Samuel Gross. On November 17, 1915, U.S. Marines captured Fort Riviere, a stronghold of the Cacos rebels. For the next nineteen years, advisers of the United States governed the country, enforced by the United States Marine Corps. The last United States Marines left the country August 15, 1934 but the National City boys controlled all Haitian financial affairs until 1947 to insure that all their loans would be paid by the Haitian people.

In May 15, 1916 Major General Smedely Butler found himself on the other side of the same island in the Dominican Republic after President Woodrow Wilson sent United States Marines into Santo Domingo. On June 1, Marines occupied Monte Cristi and Puerto Plata, and, after a brief campaign, took Arias's stronghold Santiago by the beginning of July. Wilson imposed a U.S. military government, with Rear Admiral Harry Shepard Knapp as Military Governor because Francisco Henríquez y Carvajal the Dominican Congress's duly elected President refused to meet U. S. Demands.   During the occupation the American government modernized the country's infrastructure with roads and highways, instituted the tax system, and developed primary education. Despite these reforms Domincans begrudged being controlled by a foreign power.

In 1920, U.S. authorities enacted the Land Registration Act, which displaced thousands of Dominicans because they could not produce formal land titles to their property. These properties were then confiscated by the wealthy sugar companies. By 1926, only twenty-one major estates remained, occupying an estimated 520,000 acres. Of these, twelve U.S.-owned companies owned more than 81% of this total area. The US military was used to produce more sugar profits at the expense of thousands of Dominican citizens forced from their lands. A side note to this phenomenon the American Sugar Refining Company later to become Domino Sugar and one of the first twelve companies on the Dow Jones Index was controlled by National City Bank Directors. An excerpt from the Domino Sugar company's own recorded history makes claims that it once controlled 100 percent of the American sugar market. Major General Smedely Butler came to realize why he and his marines were sent.

"Statistics:
Wholly Owned Subsidiary of Tate & Lyle plc
Incorporated: 1891 as The American Sugar Refining Company
Employees: 330
Sales: $340 million (1997 est.)
SICs: 2062 Cane Sugar Refining

Company History:

...Always at the forefront of technological developments in sugar refining, the company grew larger and larger, forcing many smaller competitors out of business. In fact, by the mid-1890s the American Sugar Refining Company was providing almost 100 percent of the refined sugar purchased by consumers across the United States. Yet when Theodore "Teddy" Roosevelt became president of the country after the assassination of William McKinley in the year 1901, Roosevelt used his "bully pulpit" and the growing

public sentiment against monopolies to enact legislation limiting the control of tobacco, sugar, petroleum, railroad, and steel manufacturing companies engaged in practices that eliminated competition within the marketplace. Suddenly, the prospect of future competition from other sugar refiners became imminent.

The astute leadership of Henry Havemeyer, however, sidestepped the problem. Henry came up with the idea of labeling the company's sugar products with a brand name, and thus Domino sugar was born when the name was applied to sugar cubes that resembled dominoes. Having a trademark name assured the company of an increased awareness in the public eye, and the company continued to maintain a stranglehold on the sugar refining business in the United States. Proof of the brand name visibility and popularity of Domino sugar was evident when, in spite of being sued by the U.S. government for monopolistic practices within the sugar industry in 1907, the company's sugar products continued to sell best with American consumers..."

Further Reading:

"American Sugar Refining Corporation," *Fortune*, February 1933, pp. 59-65, 115.
"Amstar: Two Parts Sucrose, One Part Fructose and a Heap Of Money," *Financial World*, September 1, 1976, p. 23.
"A History of Domino Sugar Corporation in New York City: 1807 to the Present," New York: Domino Sugar Corporation, 1995.
Holleran, Joan, "Sweet Success," *Beverage Industry*, April 1996

From 1927 to 1929, Major General Butler was sent to China as commander of the Marine Expeditionary Force to again protect US corporate interests. He had been there as a young marine to help quell the Boxer Rebellion in 1901. University historian David A. Wilson explains what General Butler knew.

Principles and Profits: Standard Oil Responds to Chinese Nationalism, 1925-1927 by David A. Wilson, The Pacific Historical Review, Vol. 46, No. 4 The author is affiliated with the history departments in the University of Missouri, St. Louis and Washington University.

"On March 25, 1925, The Canton government in South China notified all oil dealers in Kwangtung Province that beginning on April 1, a stamp tax of twenty cents would be levied on every five-gallon tin of kerosene. .....Standard Oil vice president Howard E. Cole and their attorney, Roland S. Morris, urged the State Department's Frank P. Lockhart to initiate military force to prevent the company's loss of $800,000 a year just in Kwangtung. ...... U.S. Marine Brigadier General Smedley Butler was sent to China to protect the lives and property of U.S. Nationals in Tientsin and offer temporary refuge for those Nationals in Tientsin. General Butler arrived with the 3rd Marine Brigade, including his aide Arthur J. Burks, my grandfather, on March 16, 1927 and disembarked at the Standard Oil dock in the Whangpoo River opposite Shanghai. They set up tents in the Standard Oil compound and that is where they stayed. Their mission was unclear. Butler, to keep the Marines from being involved with the

fighting between the two Chinese factions, attempted to maintain cordial relations with the Chinese people. His genuine respect and kindness towards the Chinese people won their appreciation and respect for him. He didn't want another Haiti-style intervention that put him into the position of defending American business interests against the native rebels and he didn't want to risk a single Marine's life for Standard Oil...."

The Plot to Seize the White House by Jules Archer, Hawthorne Books, Inc., New York 1973, pg. 93-108

"...Butler resented the use of the military to protect big business profits overseas and was very vocal about it. He publicly criticized the treatment veterans received and the "indifference of big business toward the men in uniform who had so often been called upon to spill blood for corporate profits." The presence of the Marines in China had nothing to do with the government's professed concern about the safety of Americans living in China. It was to defend Standard Oil property and profits. Vietnam War critic, David M. Shoup, future Marine Corps Commandant, reached the same conclusion – the government endangered the lives of those Marines to protect Standard Oil. In 1930, General Butler was the senior-ranking major general in the Marine Corps and the "logical choice as the next commandant" but he was passed over. Navy Secretary Charles Francis Adams and President Hoover were incensed over his very public vocalizations about using military intervention for the benefit of big business. He was an articulate, extemporaneous speaker and gave

over 1,200 speeches in over 700 cities during his speaking tour of the United States. Butler, aware of America's growing distrust and disillusionment over the reasons why the armed forces were sent overseas, really infuriated the Hoover Administration when he decided to disclose those ongoing military procedures. This was at about the same time that Hoover and the media were trying to reassure the American people that the orchestrated economic crash was nothing to worry about..."

After returning from China General Butler retired on October 1, 1931 after more than thirty-three years of service. Butler saw that American administrations had persistently cried wolf in order to use him and the youths under him to protect and augment foreign investments wrapped in the flag. He was worn out from his speaking engagements and entered the Philadelphia Naval Hospital for a rest and examination. Just as America's political leaders were gearing up for World War II, General Butler died unexpectedly on June 21, 1940 at the Naval Hospital in Philadelphia at the age of 58.

What would the framers of the Constitution and the Bill of Rights have done differently if they had been able to foresee the expansion of the American War complex? What about the great wealth that it would be able to bestow on those who learned how to control it secrets? Would they have added principles to the articles that would insure that our military would not be called upon by our government to pillage and spoil the natural resources of foreign lands for our elite? Would they have written amendments that would curtail the use of military power against nations that pose no threat to our shores? Or did they believe that as Americans we would extend the courtesies found in the Bill of rights to people in other nations of the world using these same principles in our dealing with foreign people?

The Founding Fathers cannot be called upon to undo the last centuries slow dismantling of their doctrines of Life, Liberty and the Pursuit of Happiness. The people of America will have to arm themselves with the knowledge of history to truly understand what has happened and how we have arrived at the challenges that we face today. It is our responsibility to identify courageous men and women who would rise to the seemingly insurmountable confrontations facing our nation. To find men and women who would operate outside the normal sphere of political posturing. Leaders that would press towards the reforming of a government that is completely insane. Leaders like General Butler not afraid to oppose the special interests groups that make up our military complex and speak out against their deceit. Brave men that can identify the break downs in the law making processes that make it possible for influences outside of our government to grab control and use it to benefit their own distorted goals. Americans can only vote good leaders into our government if they have a full understanding of the history of the last centuries. Without it we are led by every whim of the special interests that control our major news media and decisions are made by the fifteen second sound bites they feed us day in and day out. The challenge to every American today that cares about the future of our country is to turn off the sound bites and start researching true history. The answers to our problems lie somewhere in that research.

Chapter 5

"The Governing of our Government"

"SIR, The most successful deluders and oppressors of mankind have always acted in masquerade; and when the blackest villainies are meant, the most opposite spirit is pretended, Vice acts with security, and often with reputation, under the Vail of virtue."

Cato's Letters
Thomas Gordon
(December 31, 1720)

The concentration of corporate greed by the end of the nineteenth century gave rise to a consolidation of money, business and banking. In a time that was void of antitrust laws corporations, banks and individuals formed monopolies to eliminate all competition. They deliberately consolidated their efforts using collusion and lobbying to further their control of the markets. By the beginning of the twentieth century most industries in the United States were controlled by a small group. Those who controlled their industries were brought together by the common interest in the banking world that further consolidated them into a single entity controlled by a handful of men. Men like JP Morgan, John Rockefeller, Paul Warburg, Jacob Schiff, Benjamin Strong and Andrew Carnegie were successful in monopolizing practically the entire country. The two largest banks of the time Kuhn Loeb and company and the National City Bank were the instruments of unification.

With their consolidated power they preceded to influence lawmakers. They changed the laws in their favor so they could hold onto to this power indefinitely. The backlash of this phenomenon created the progressive labor movement to combat the corporate takeover. The struggle between the corporate elite and the labor movement was the political catalyst that drove public sentiment in the newspapers. The corporatists were able to rig elections in their favor. They used the anger of the people to further enact legislation that would line their pockets and remove liberties from the American people.

Legislators like Charles Lindberg Sr. Congressman from Minnesota and Senator Robert M. LaFollete of Wisconsin were great men who saw the coming dangers of the corporate consolidations and the effect this would have on our Constitution and Bill of rights. They fought in the congress to expose this evil but their voices fell on the deaf ears of a congress that had been hypnotized by big business.

"There is a man-made god that controls the social and industrial system that governs us. We know him as the "Money Trust." He is offended if given or called by his true name, and being jealous of his power, he opposed an investigation of its sources. At the present time he has an almost illimitable influence upon our daily actions and is seeking to increase it by framing new currency and banking laws to suit his purposes."

US Congressman Charles Lindbergh Sr. Minnesota – Banking and Currency and the Money Trust National Capitol Press Inc. copyright 1913

Congressman Lindbergh introduced a resolution to the congress for an investigation of Wall Street. He believed through mergers, trusts and acquisitions of dominant corporations that the power of the financial world was being consolidated for the purpose of control. With the support of Senator Robert M LaFollette of Wisconsin also an open opponent of the "Money Trust" they succeeded in bringing about the Subcommittee of the Committee on Banking and Currency headed by Representative Arsene Pujo of Louisiana. This became known as the Pujo Committee.

The investigation began in May of 1912 and continued until January 1913. The Pujo Committee Report concluded that a community of influential financial leaders had gained control of major manufacturing, transportation, mining, telecommunications and the financial markets of the United States. The report also concluded eighteen different major financial corporations were under control of a cartel lead by J.P Morgan, George F Baker and James Stillman. The report included individual bankers Paul Warburg, Jacob H. Schiff, Felix M. Warburg, Frank E. Peabody, William Rockefeller and Benjamin Strong, Jr. which had influence over $22 billion in resources and capitalization controlled through 341 directorships held in 112 corporations by members of the empire headed by J.P. Morgan. Without the committees right to access the books on the national banks the committee reported that "There is no agreement existing among these men that is in violation of the law." Although Lindbergh's assertions proved to be correct the lack of sufficient legislation to control such actions had yet to be created. The following reprinted excerpt is reprinted to show you what was found to be absolutely true by the legislator's investigation.

Senator Robert M LaFollette wrote about the findings in a book "Great Leaders and National Issues of 1912" Chapter 25.

"CONTROL OF BUSINESS BY A FEW MEN - GROWTH OF FINANCIAL BANKING - THE STANDARD OIL AND MORGAN GROUPS - CONNECTIONS OF NATIONAL CITY DIRECTORS - RESERVES ARE MASSED IN NEW YORK-EVIDENCE OF SPECULATION BY BANKS - FINANCIAL BANKING SUPPLANTING COMMERCIAL BANKING

"In making these reorganizations the opportunity for a large paper capitalization offered too great a temptation to be resisted. This was but the first stage in the creation of fictitious wealth. *The success of these organizations led quickly on to a consolidation of combined industries until a mere handful of men controlled the industrial production of the country.*

Control of Business by a Few Men

I have compiled a list of about one hundred men with their directorships in the great corporate business enterprises of the United States. It furnishes indisputable proof of the community of interest that controls the industrial life of the country.

The Standard Oil and Morgan Groups

The bare names of the directors of two great bank groups the Standard Oil group and the Morgan group given in connection with their other business associations is all the evidence that need be offered of the absolute community of interest between banks railroads and all the great industries. There are twenty three directors of the National City Bank, "Standard Oil". There are thirty nine directors of the National Bank of Commerce, "Morgan". *Examination of these directorates shows that the two groups are being knit together in business associations suggesting their ultimate unification.* Subject to personal differences which may arise between powerful individuals of these different groups resulting in occasional collision they are practically a monopoly and as far as the public is concerned practically one group. The business partner of the head of the Morgan group is found on the directorate of the chief financial institution which heads the Standard Oil group. And one of the leading directors of the National City Bank, Standard Oil is a member of the board of directors of the principal financial institution in the Morgan group. The directors of the leading organizations comprising the two principal groups are bound together in mutual interest as shareholders in the various transportation franchise and industrial concerns which have been financed by one or the other of the groups in recent years.

Connections of National City Directors

Fourteen of the directors of the National City Bank are at the head of fourteen great combinations representing thirty eight per cent of the capitalization of all the industrial trusts of the country. The railroad lines represented on the board of this one bank cover the country like a network. Chief among them are the Lackawanna, the Chicago, Burlington and Quincy, the Union Pacific, the Alton, the Missouri Pacific, the Chicago, Milwaukee and St Paul, the Chicago and Northwestern, the Rock Island, the Denver and Rio Grande, the Mexican National, the Baltimore and Ohio, the Northern Pacific, the New York Central the Texas and Pacific, the Erie, the New York, New Haven and Hartford, the Delaware and Hudson, the Illinois Central the Manhattan, Elevated of New York City and the rapid transit lines of Brooklyn. These same twenty three directors through their various connections represent more than 350 other banks trust companies railroads and industrial corporations with an aggregate capitalization of more than twelve thousand million dollars. That is a part only of what is behind the directorate of the National City Bank of New York the head of only one of these groups.

Reserves are Massed in New York

It was inevitable that this massing of banking power should attract to itself the resources of other banks throughout the country. Capital attracts capital. It inspires confidence. It appeals to the imagination. Added to this the forces back of these controlling groups could offer tempting interest rates **and finally the federal legislation would almost seem to have been enacted to augment this power.** The law providing that fifteen per cent of the deposits of a country bank should be held for the protection of its depositors conveniently permits three fifths of the amount to be deposited in reserve city banks and of the twenty five per cent of reserve for the protection of depositors in reserve city banks one half may be deposited with central reserve city banks. As there are but three central reserve cities one of which of course is New York City the alluring interest rates which these all powerful groups could offer inevitably tended to draw the great proportion of lawful reserves subject to transfer from the country and reserve banks. Consider the number of country banks for which these larger banks are the approved reserve agents and the way the system has been worked to gather up the money of the country by these big group banks can be understood. *One Standard Oil bank is approved agent to receive deposits of lawful money reserves from 1,071 national banks scattered over the country. Another bank of the same group receives reserve deposits from 1,802 country banks and another from 478. A leading Morgan group bank receives deposits from 909 outside banks and another from 615 and still another from 1,233.* The power which the New York banks derive through these vast accumulations of the resources of other national banks strengthens their position so that they could draw in the surplus money of all the other financial institutions of the country, state, private and savings banks and trust companies.

Financial Banking Supplanting Commercial Banking

The plain truth is that legitimate commercial banking is being eaten up by financial banking. The greatest banks of the financial center of the country have ceased to be agents of commerce and have become primarily agencies of promotion and speculation. *By merging the largest banks trust companies and insurance companies masses of capital have been brought under one management to be employed not as the servant of commerce but as its master, not to supply legitimate business and to facilitate exchange but to subordinate the commercial demands of the country upon the banks to call loans in Wall Street and to finance industrial organizations always speculative and often unlawful in character.* Trained men who a dozen years ago stood first among the bankers of the world as heads of the greatest banks of New York City are in the main either displaced or do the bidding of men who are not bankers but masters of organization. With this enormous concentration of business it is possible to create artificially periods of prosperity and periods of panic. Prices can be lowered or advanced at the will of the System. When the farmer must move his crops a scarcity of money may be created and prices lowered. When the crop passes into the control of the speculator the artificial stringency may be relieved and prices advanced and the illegitimate profit raked off the agricultural industry may be pocketed in Wall Street. *If an effort is made to compel any one of these great interests to obey the law it is easy for them to enter a conspiracy to destroy whoever may be responsible for the undertaking.* The business of the country is transacted by corporations and combinations of corporations. The control of corporations rests of necessity with a board of directors the executive committee and the officers of the organization. It is therefore only necessary to take the great controlling transportation and business organizations of the country analyze the directorates and the truth is ascertained."

JP Morgan Cartoon

The absurdity of the Pujo Committee was that not a single well-known opponent of the money trust would be allowed to appear or testify. Lead Council Samuel Untermyer ignored Senator LaFollette and Congressman Charles Augustus Lindbergh. Although the "Money Trust" was found to exist by the commission the only thing the commission accomplished was to play right into the hands of the men who controlled the "Money Trust". When the hearings were over, the bankers and their subsidized newspapers claimed that the only way to break this monopoly was to enact the banking and currency legislation now being proposed to Congress, the Federal Reserve Act. What the unsuspecting public was unaware of was that this course of action was planned to perfection by those who controlled the "Money Trust" and the ultimate plundering mechanism was about to be created.

The Jekyll Island Expedition

One evening in early November 1910, Kuhn, Loeb, and Co. partner and Director of Wells Fargo & Company Paul M. Warburg along with Senator Nelson Aldrich of Rhode Island, his personal secretary Arthur Shelton, former Harvard University professor of economics Dr. A. Piatt Andrew, J.P. Morgan & Co. partner Henry P. Davison, J.P. Morgan partner; Benjamin Strong, vice president of Banker's Trust Co and National City Bank president Frank A. Vanderlip from New York quietly boarded Sen. Aldrich's private railway car, ostensibly for a trip south to an exclusive hunting club owned by J.P. Morgan on an island off the coast of Georgia. Senator Aldrich had close ties with J. P. Morgan and other important bankers, and his eldest daughter's marriage to John D. Rockefeller Jr. proves the associations. It is proposed that these men were in control of one quarter of the wealth of America. Senator Aldrich was an insider of the "Money Trust" and was given the commission by the US Congress to travel to Europe to study the central banking systems in Europe. These men at Jekyll Island aided in drafting the report that was to be presented to the congress. The report was submitted to Congress on January 9, 1912. In this report there were recommendations and draft legislation with 59 sections, for proposed changes in U.S. banking and currency laws. The proposed legislation was known as the Aldrich Plan. The plan called for the establishment of a National Reserve Association with 15 regional district branches and 46 geographically dispersed directors primarily from the banking profession. The Reserve Association would make emergency loans to member banks, create money, and act as the fiscal agent for the U.S. government. State and nationally chartered banks would have the option of subscribing to specified stock in their local association branch.

With the Senators relationships to the New York Bankers and the fact that the Aldrich plan essentially gave full control of this system to private bankers, there was strong opposition to it because of fears that it would become a tool of certain rich and powerful financiers in New York City. It became known as the Wall Street Plan. The powers at the top had to come up with a better plan to get their way. The presidential Campaign of 1912 would be crucial to meet their ends. No expense was to be spared to get the right politicians in place for the battle and the 1912 campaign showed to be one of the most ambiguous upsets in the History of American elections.

William Howard Taft the Republican was at the time blessed with a prosperous economy. The Republican Party controlled both the house and the Senate. The Democratic challenger, Woodrow Wilson, Governor of New Jersey had very little support but the democratic platform had their own version of the Aldrich Plan named the Federal Reserve Act. Except for the name the plans were Identical. In an odd turn of events Theodore Roosevelt announced he would run for President as a third party candidate. As a republican ex-president he was sure to take a substantial amount of votes from Taft. As it came to pass Woodrow Wilson became President with only 41.8 % of the vote while Taft and Roosevelt split the remaining 58%. The result was that a democratic congress and a democratic president were elected in 1912 to get the central bank legislation passed. It seems probable that the identification of the Aldrich Plan as a Wall Street operation predicted that it would have a difficult passage through congress, as the democrats would solidly oppose it, whereas a successful democratic candidate, supported by a democratic congress, would be able to pass the central bank plan. The Federal Reserve Act was enacted December 23, 1913 thus creating the Federal Reserve System, the central banking system of the United States of America, and granted it the legal authority to issue legal tender. It is important to note that the Federal Reserve is not Federal and it is not a reserve it is a private bank held by stockholders of which the American people are not allowed to know who owns this stock. The Act was signed into law by President Woodrow Wilson. This gave the private bankers the power they craved to create money out of thin air. Then loan this money to the Federal government collecting interest on the money they created from nothing. The power to regulate interest rates, the influence to inflate or deflate the economy of the US at will and ultimately to set up a secret government to control the United States Government and the people it seeks to protect.

Alfred Crozier, in his book written in 1911, U.S. Money vs. Corporation Currency attacked the Aldrich plan as a Wall Street instrument, and he pointed out that when our government had to issue money based on privately owned securities, we were no longer a free nation. Crozier testified before the Senate Committee:

"It should prohibit the granting or calling in of loans for the purpose of influencing quotation prices of securities and the contracting of loans or increasing interest rates in concert by the banks to influence public opinion or the action of any legislative body. Within recent months, William McAdoo, Secretary of the Treasury of the United States was reported in the open press as charging specifically that there was a conspiracy among certain of the large banking interests to put a contraction upon the currency and to raise interest rates for the sake of making the public force Congress into passing currency legislation desired by those interests. The so-called administration currency bill grants just what Wall Street and the big banks for twenty-five years have been striving for, that is, **PRIVATE INSTEAD OF PUBLIC CONTROL OF CURRENCY. It does this as completely as the Aldrich Bill. Both measures rob the government and the people of all effective control over the public's money, and vest in the banks exclusively the dangerous power to make money among the people scarce or plenty.** *The Aldrich Bill puts this power in one central bank. The Administration Bill puts it in twelve regional central banks, all owned exclusively by the identical private interests that would have owned and operated the Aldrich Bank. President Garfield shortly before his assassination declared that whoever controls the supply of currency would control the business and activities of*

the people. Thomas Jefferson warned us a hundred years ago that a private central bank issuing the public currency was a greater menace to the liberties of the people than a standing army."

On December 23, 1913 the citizens of the United States of America were victims of the plot hatched in the back halls of Wall Street by the titans of American banking. Woodrow Wilson and his Wall Street backed congress despite the warnings of our Founding Fathers sold out the country, the people, the Constitution, the Bill of Rights and the memory of all the men who died in the revolutionary war to bring us freedom. President Woodrow Wilson, after having broken campaign promises and betrayed his country by signing into law the Federal Reserve Act actually showed regret when he said,

"I am a most unhappy man. I have unwittingly ruined my country.

A great industrial nation is controlled by its system of credit. Our system of credit is concentrated. The growth of the nation therefore, and all our activities, are in the hands of a few men. We have come to be one of the worst ruled, one of the most completely controlled and dominated Governments in the civilized world. No longer a Government by free opinion, no longer a Government by conviction and the vote of the majority, but a Government by the opinion and duress of a small group of dominant men."

Wilson declared the sentiments of the opponents of the central banking system. They were battling against the loss of liberty and property. He came to realize that his administration had unleashed an eminently destructive financial weapon of mass destruction on the world and put it in the hands of men. His words "worst ruled", "completely controlled" and "dominated government" should make the hair stand up on the back of the necks of every patriotic American.

The Founding Fathers were not unfamiliar with central banking systems used by European nations to enslave their subjects and take away their liberties and properties. Thomas Jefferson speaking on the first attempt to establish a central bank in America:

"The system of banking is a blot left in all our Constitutions, which, if not covered, will end in their destruction. I sincerely believe that banking institutions are more dangerous than standing armies; and that the principle of spending money to be paid by posterity is but swindling futurity on a large scale."

"The end of democracy, and the defeat of the American revolution will occur when government falls into the hands of the lending institutions and moneyed incorporations."

"If the people ever allow the banks to issue their currency, the banks and corporations which will grow up around them will deprive the people of all property, until their children wake up homeless on the continent their fathers conquered."

"Paper is poverty... It is not money, but the ghost of money."

"There is an artificial aristocracy, founded on birth and privilege, without virtue or talents... The artificial aristocracy is a mischievous ingredient in government, and provisions should be made to prevent its ascendency."

"The bank of the United States is one of the most deadly hostilities existing against the principles and form of our Constitution. I deem no government safe which is under the vassalage of any self-constituted authorities, or any other authority than that of the nation, or its regular functionaries. What an obstruction could not this bank of the United States, with all its branch banks, be in a time of war? It might dictate to us the peace we should accept, or it might withdraw its aid. Ought we then to give further growth to an institution so powerful, so hostile?"

Jefferson spoke of the central bank as more destructive than a standing army. It will swindle our future from us. It will end the republic, defeat the American Revolution, will have us wake up homeless on the continent our fathers conquered, existing against the principles and form of the Constitution, and will dictate War. Do you think he would have opposed the Federal Reserve Act of 1913 if he had a vote? He probably would have chased everyone out of the Congress with a large wooden club. His contemporary James Madison speaking on the first attempt to establish a central bank in America called them money changers an analogy from the New Testament speaking of the men who were thrown out of the temple in Jerusalem by Christ with a whip for using it to swindle the people.

"History records that the money changers have used every form of abuse, intrigue, deceit and violent means possible, to maintain their control over governments, by controlling money and its issuance."

GENERAL JACKSON SLAYING THE MANY HEADED MONSTER.

Andrew Jackson speaking on the second attempt to establish a central bank in America, of which he succeeded to abolish, said,

"If congress has the right under the Constitution to issue paper money, it was given them to use themselves, not to be delegated to individuals or corporations."

"I am one of those who do not believe that a national debt is a national blessing, but rather a curse to a republic, inasmuch as it is calculated to raise around the administration a monied aristocracy dangerous to the liberties of the country."

"You are a den of vipers and thieves. I intend to rout you out, and by the Eternal god, I will rout you out!"

Jackson was adamant that the right to issue money was reserved to the government not private banks. He believed a national debt was a detriment to society that it would give rise to an aristocracy that would be dangerous to liberty. He spent the better part of his Presidency closing down the second bank of the United States an earlier attempt at a central bank. I am sure he would also have voted no to the Federal Reserve Act.

Abraham Lincoln speaking on the third attempt to establish a central bank in America,

"The money powers prey on the nation in times of peace and conspire against it in times of adversity. The banking powers are more despotic than monarchy, more insolent than autocracy, more selfish than bureaucracy. They denounce as public enemy's all who question their methods or throw light upon their crimes.

I have two great enemies, the Southern Army in front of me, and the bankers in the rear. Of the two, the one at my rear is my greatest foe. As a most undesirable consequence of the war, corporations have been enthroned, and an era of corruption in high places will follow. The money power will endeavor to prolong its reign by working upon the prejudices of the people until the wealth is aggregated in the hands of a few, and the Republic is destroyed."

How is it that every former great American Leader before 1900 understood the absolute power of money? Are we to believe that somehow the leaders after 1900 became uninformed or were uneducated as to the struggles that the former administrators faced? Abraham Lincoln called the banking powers despotic, insolent and selfish he regarded them a greater foe than the armies of the south but somehow less than 50 years after he said that these same bankers were given the key to the city by congress.

US Congressman, Louis T. McFadden, Pennsylvania (Congressional Record, June 15, 1934):

"Every effort has been made by the Federal Reserve Board to conceal its power. But the truth is the Federal Reserve Board has usurped the government of the United States.

It controls everything here; and it controls our foreign relations. It makes or breaks governments at will. **No man, and no body of men, is more entrenched in power than the arrogant credit monopoly which operates the Federal Reserve Board and Federal Reserve Banks.**

These evil-doers have robbed the country of more than enough money to pay the national debt. **What the National Government has permitted the Federal Reserve Board to steal from the people should now be returned to the people.** *The people have a valid claim against the Federal Reserve Board and the Federal Reserve Banks. If that claim is enforced, Americans will not need to stand in bread lines. Homes will be saved. Families will be kept.*

What is needed here is a return to the Constitution of the United States. *The old struggle that was fought out here in Jackson's day must be fought over again.*

The Federal Reserve Act should be repealed; *and the Federal Reserve Banks -- having violated their charters -- should be liquidated immediately.* **Faithless government officers who have violated their oaths of office should be impeached and brought to trial.**

Unless this is done by us, I predict the American people -- outraged, robbed, pillaged, insulted, and betrayed as they are in their own land -- will rise in their wrath and send a President here who WILL sweep the money changers from the temple."

Money is the ruling power behind everything those who have the gold make the rules. We cannot through the channels of the election process pretend to believe that we can remedy the ills of society by the authorized Constitutional government while it is being controlled by an invisible government. Our first attempt at transforming our nation back to the traditions and principles of the men who founded the nation is eradicating completely the private banking control that has plagued America for the last 97 years in the form of the Federal Reserve Act of destruction.

In a prophetic Cato Letter written almost three hundred years ago by John Trenchard we see a haunting parallel in the events facing America today. (Reproduced in its entirety emphasis mine)

What Measures are actually taken by wicked and desperate Ministers to ruin and enslave their Country

Cato's Letter No. 17
John Trenchard (February 18, 1721)

"*SIR, As under the best princes, and the best servants to princes alone, it is safe to speak what is true of the worst; so, according to my former promise to the publick, I shall take the advantage of our excellent King's most gentle government, and the virtuous administration of an uncorrupt ministry, to warn mankind against the mischiefs which may hereafter be dreaded from corrupt ones. It is too true, that every country in the world has sometimes groaned under that heavy misfortune, and our own as much as any; though I cannot allow it to be true, what Monsieur de Witt has long since observed, that the English court has always been the most thievish court in Europe.*

*Few men have been desperate enough to attack openly, and barefaced, the liberties of a free people. Such avowed conspirators can rarely succeed: The attempt would destroy itself. Even when the enterprize is begun and visible, the end must be hid, or denied. **It is the business and policy of traitors, so to disguise their treason with plausible names**, and so to recommend it with popular and bewitching colours, that they themselves shall be adored, while their work is detested, and yet carried on by those that detest it.*

Thus one nation has been surrendered to another under the fair name of mutual alliance: The fortresses of a nation have been given up, or attempted to be given up, under the frugal notion of saving charges to a nation; and commonwealths have been trepanned into slavery, by troops raised or increased to defend them from slavery.

*It may therefore be of service to the world, **to show what measures have been taken by corrupt ministers**, in some of our neighbouring countries, to ruin and enslave the people over whom they presided; to shew by what steps and gradations of mischief nations have been undone, and consequently what methods may be hereafter taken to undo others: And this subject I rather choose, because my countrymen may be the more sensible of, and know how to value the inestimable blessing of living under the best prince, and the best established government in the universe, where we have none of these things to fear.*

*Such traitors will probably **endeavour first to get their prince into their possession**, and, like Sejanus, shut him up in a little island, or perhaps make him a prisoner in his court; whilst, with full range, they devour his dominions, and **plunder his subjects**. When he is thus secluded from the access of his friends, and* the knowledge of his affairs, he must be content with such misrepresentations as they shall find expedient to give him. False cases will be stated, to justify wicked counsel; wicked counsel will be given, to procure unjust orders. He will be made to **mistake his foes for his friends, his friends for his foes**; and to believe that his affairs are in the highest prosperity, when they are in the greatest distress; and that publick matters go on in the greatest harmony, when they are in the utmost confusion.

They will be ever contriving and forming wicked and dangerous **projects, to make the people poor, and themselves rich**; well knowing that dominion follows property; that where there are wealth and power, **there will be always crowds of servile dependents**; and that, on the contrary, poverty dejects the mind, **fashions it to slavery**, and renders it unequal to any generous undertaking, and incapable of opposing any bold usurpation. They will **squander away the publick money** in wanton presents to minions, and their creatures of pleasure or of burden, or in **pensions to mercenary and worthless men and women**, for vile ends and traitorous purposes.

They will **engage their country in ridiculous, expensive, fantastical wars,** to keep the minds of men in continual hurry and agitation, and under constant fears and alarms; and, by such means, deprive them both of leisure and inclination to look into publick miscarriages. Men, on the contrary, will, instead of such inspection, be disposed to fall into all measures offered, seemingly, **for their defence, and <u>will agree to every wild demand</u>** made by those who are betraying **them.**

When they have served their ends by such wars, or have other motives to make peace, they will have no *view to the publick interest; but will often, to procure such peace, deliver up the strong-holds of their country, or its colonies for trade, to open enemies, suspected friends, or dangerous neighbours, that they may not be interrupted in their domestick designs.*

*They will **create parties in the commonwealth**, or keep them up where they already are; and, **by playing them by turns upon each other, will rule both**. By making the Guelfs afraid of the Ghibelines, and these afraid of the Guelfs, they will make themselves the mediums and balance between the two factions; and both factions, in their turns, the props of their authority, and the instruments of their designs.*

*They will not suffer any men, who have once tasted of authority, though personally their enemies, and whose posts they enjoy, to be called to an account for past crimes, though ever so enormous. They will make no such precedents for their own punishment; nor censure treason, which they intend to commit. On the contrary, they will form new conspiracies, and invent new fences for their own impunity and protection; and endeavour to engage such numbers in their guilt, as to **set themselves above all fear of punishment**.*

*They will prefer worthless and wicked men, and **not suffer a man of knowledge or honesty to come near them**, or enjoy a post under them. They will **disgrace men of virtue**, and ridicule virtue itself, and **laugh at publick spirit**. They will put men into employments, without any regard to the qualifications for those employments, or indeed to any qualifications at all, but as they contribute to their designs, and shew a stupid alacrity to do what they are bid. They must be either fools or beggars; either void of capacity to discover their intrigues, or of credit and inclination to disappoint them.*

They will promote luxury, idleness, and expence, *and a general depravation of manners, by their own example, as well as by connivance and publick encouragement. This will not only divert men's thoughts from examining their behaviour and politicks, but likewise let them loose from all the restraints of private and publick virtue.* ***From immorality and excesses they will fall into necessity; and from thence into a servile dependence upon power.***

In order to this, they will bring into fashion gaming, drunkenness, gluttony, and profuse and costly dress. They will debauch their country with foreign vices, and foreign instruments of vicious pleasures; and will contrive and encourage publick revels, nightly disguises, and debauched mummeries.

They will, by all practicable means of oppression, provoke the people to disaffection; and then make that disaffection an argument for new oppression, for not trusting them any further, and for keeping up troops; and, in fine, for depriving them of liberties and privileges, to which they are entitled by their birth, and the laws of their country.

If such measures should ever be taken in any free country, where the people choose deputies to represent them, then they will endeavour to bribe the electors in the choice of their representatives, and so to get a council of their own creatures; and where they cannot succeed with the electors, they will endeavour to corrupt the deputies after they are chosen, with the money given for the publick defence; and to draw into the perpetration of their crimes those very men, from whom the betrayed people expect the redress of their grievances, and the punishment of those crimes. And when they have thus made the representatives of the people afraid of the people, and the people afraid of their representatives; then they will endeavour to persuade those deputies to seize the government to themselves, and not to trust their principals any longer with the power of resenting their treachery and ill-usage, and of sending honester and wiser men in their room.

But if the constitution should be so stubbornly framed, that it will still preserve itself and the people's liberties, in spite of all villainous contrivances to destroy both; then must the constitution itself be attacked and broken, because it will not bend. There must be an endeavour, under some pretence of publick good, to alter a balance of the government, and to get it into the sole power of their creatures, and of such who will have constantly an interest distinct from that of the body of the people.

But if all these schemes for the ruin of the publick, and their own impunity, should fail them; and the worthy patriots of a free country should prove obstinate in defence of their country, and resolve to call its betrayers to a strict account; there is then but one thing left for such traitors to do; namely, to veer about, and, **by joining with the enemy of their prince and country, complete their treason.**

I have somewhere read of a favourite and first minister to a neighbouring prince, long since dead, who played his part so well, that, though he had, by his evil counsels, raised a rebellion, and a contest for the crown; yet he **preserved himself a resource, whoever got the better:** *If his old master succeeded, then this Achitophel, by the help of a baffled rebellion, ever favourable to princes, had the glory of fixing his master in absolute power: But, as his brave rival got the day, Achitophel had the merit of betraying his old master to plead; and was accordingly taken into favour.*

Happy therefore, thrice happy, are we, who can be unconcerned spectators of the miseries which the greatest part of Europe is reduced to suffer, **having lost their liberties by the intrigues and wickedness of those whom they trusted;** *whilst we continue in full enjoyment of ours, and can be in no danger of losing them, while we have so excellent a King, assisted and obeyed by so wise a Parliament."*

This was written in 1721 but it seems like it could be an American political commentary in 2011.

Chapter 6

"Can the leech be removed without killing the host?"

Money, one of the most misapprehended subjects of all time. What is money? Money is any good that is widely used and accepted in transactions involving the transfer of goods and services from one person to another. In history many commodities were considered money such as; seashells, blankets, livestock, tobacco more common were things like precious gems, silver and gold. There were obvious problems with commodities being used for money. For instance, the inability to use a horse to make a purchase for something that was worth less than the horse. You would have to cut the horse into smaller parts to match the value of the product you were buying; of course that was not an option. Gold and silver coins of different weights were used to remedy the problems with other types of money. When it came to the drafting of our Constitution the Framers gave the federal government on behalf of the people certain privileges concerning the creation of money to be used in America for commerce. Article 1, Section 8 states;

"The Congress shall have the power...To coin Money, regulate the Value thereof, and of foreign Coin, and fix the Standard of Weights and Measures;"

Article 1, Section 10 states;

No State shall enter into any Treaty, Alliance, or Confederation; grant Letters of Marque and Reprisal;

coin Money; emit Bills of Credit; make any Thing but gold and silver Coin a Tender in Payment of Debts;"

There is no other mention of money found in the Constitution. The Founding Fathers gave the federal government what they felt was sufficient functions for the conducting of commerce. These functions were:
1. Coin money.
2. Regulate the value of the coins
3. Regulate the value of foreign coins
4. Create the standard by which the coins are measured

The Constitution also made it clear that the States:
1. Were not to coin money
2. Were not to emit bills of credit
3. Were only to accept gold and silver coin as legal tender.

There are only three types of money in the world; commodity money, fiduciary money and fiat money. Commodity money is gold and silver coins. There are other commodities that have been used but gold and silver remains the most common. Fiduciary money is a certificate that promises to pay the bearer on demand a certain amount of commodity money. The government of the United States issued certificates that were backed by silver and gold in the treasury. The Silver Certificates stated,

"THIS CERTIFIES THAT THERE IS ON DEPOSIT IN THE TREASURY OF THE UNITED STATES OF AMERICA "some number" DOLLARS IN SILVER PAYABLE TO THE BEARER ON DEMAND".

The amount of silver redeemable was approved in Section 9 of the 1792 Coinage Act which states that a dollar is equivalent to 371.25 grains of pure silver. One troy ounce is equal to 480 troy grains. Higher denominations were gold certificates. The bearer could redeem his/her certificate for gold. Under the same Section 9 of the 1792 Coinage Act, a dollar was equivalent to 24.75 grains of pure gold. Fiat money, on the other hand, is used to mean any money declared by a government to be legal tender which is neither legally convertible to any other thing, nor fixed in value in terms of any objective standard. The term derives from the Latin fiat, meaning "let it be done". This is the money we use today and on the bills it states

"THIS NOTE IS LEGAL TENDER FOR ALL DEBTS PUBLIC AND PRIVATE"

The major differences in the types of money are first, in their ability to retain value and second the trust given to them by the party to whom must accept it. To grasp the difference between fiat money and commodity money all you have to do is look at the cost of products throughout history. In 1960 you could purchase a gallon of regular gasoline for .25 cents if you used a silver dollar coin in 1960 you would have received 4 gallons of gasoline. At 3 dollars a gallon today (fiat money) that same silver dollar will get you 13 gallons of gasoline because the value of the silver dollar today is about $39 dollars in fiat money. The value of commodity remains constant over the years while fiat money loses its value due to a phenomenon known as inflation. People mistakenly think of inflation as the rising of prices on goods. Remember that goods are commodities and commodities retain their value.

The amount of gold or silver used to purchase other commodities such as; oil, wheat, tobacco, livestock etc. has not changed over the course of centuries. The amount of silver you would have used in 1790 to purchase a commodity would get you the same commodity today. Inflation therefore is not the rising of the price of the commodity but the devaluation of the fiat money against the commodity.

To fully understand why our money today loses its value a clear description of the nation's financial history must be grasped. The Constitution grants the government the power to collect taxes and borrow on the good faith of the federal government. Article 1

section 8 states, *"The Congress shall have Power To lay and collect Taxes, Duties, Imposts and Excises, to pay the Debts and provide for the common Defence and general Welfare of the United States; but all Duties, Imposts and Excises shall be uniform throughout the United States;....* Without revenue the government would not be able to operate and although no one likes to pay taxes everyone must agree that a certain amount is absolutely necessary for social order.

During the early years of the nation several attempts at creating a central bank were met with defeat as the Founding Fathers were opposed to debt. They believed it to be of the utmost importance to national security for the country to operate in the black. Andrew Jackson the only president to balance the budget also fought to close down the Second Bank of the United States. He called the administrators of the bank a den of vipers and thieves. Andrew Jackson was succeeded by President Martin Van Buren who also rejected suggestions for a central bank. He proposed instead the creation of a sub-Treasury system whereby the Treasury would require payment in gold and silver and collect its revenues directly, rather than through private financial intermediaries.

Van Buren hoped to advance the cause of hard money by completely separating the federal government from the banks. The Independent Treasury Act separated the Treasury from the banking system. The act instructed the Treasury Department "to keep safely, without loaning, using, depositing in banks" all the money it collected. All transactions with the Treasury were to be settled in either money or Treasury notes. For the next 67 years, the United States financed itself using the Independent Treasury system. Prices were stable, the Federal government was small, and the standard of living improved dramatically during this period. The only disruption to the system occurred during the Civil War. To finance the war Abraham Lincoln persuaded the congress to print a limited amount of fiat money which became known as the greenback. They reached a circulation of approximately $500,000,000 but by the end of the war they were trading at half their face value in silver or gold. However, things were quickly restored once the war ended. The United States government financed itself, **without a central bank**, for more than half-a-century!

Until this time inflation was a non issue because the financial standard of the government was based on commodity money (gold and silver) and fiduciary money (backed by the gold standard) which retain their value. The passing of the Federal Reserve Act of 1913 was to change the mechanism of the commercial structure of the United States. The new mechanism is elaborate and must be dissected piece by piece to be apprehended. The Federal Reserve consists of the following:

1. The Federal Reserve Board of Governors
   a. Seven Men
   b. Appointed by the President
   c. Confirmed by the Senate
   d. Serve for 14 years
2. The Federal Open Market Committee (FOMC)
   a. Conducts the operations of the central banks buying and selling of Treasury Securities
   b. Directs operations undertaken by the Federal Reserve System in foreign exchange markets
3. Twelve Private Regional Banks
   a. New York

      b. Boston
      c. Philadelphia
      d. Cleveland
      e. Richmond
      f. Atlanta
      g. Chicago
      h. St. Louis
      i. Minneapolis
      j. Kansa City
      k. Dallas
      l. San Francisco

4. Member Banks
      a. Commercial
      b. Private

The twelve private Federal Reserve Banks act as banks to the bankers. The twelve private Federal Reserve banks together divide the nation into twelve districts, created by the Federal Reserve Act of 1913. Each private Federal Reserve Bank is responsible for the regulation of the commercial banks within its own particular district. Monetary policy and bank regulations are controlled by the chairman and board of governors to keep the districts working in unison. The act also mandated that all nationally chartered banks were to become members of the Federal Reserve and were forced to purchase stock in the Federal Reserve. Each district bank is set up like a corporation with a president and board of directors. It is important to remember the central bank is not a government bank, it is a private corporation owned by stock holders. The Federal Reserve Banks set up accounts for the commercial member banks and institutions in their districts to maintain their deposits under detailed banking regulations. Only member banking institutions and the US government are eligible to maintain accounts or receive loans from the central banks. Neither Private Citizens nor other kinds of non-bank commercial enterprises are allowed to participate.

Several definitions of terms are necessary to complete the discussion of the central bank mechanism that influences inflation;

- *Money Supply*
- *Currency*
- *Demand deposits*
- *Reserves*
- *Fractional reserve banking*

Money supply is the term used to describe the total amount of money claimed to exist in a country at a particular point in time. It includes currency outstanding and deposits in banks.

Currency is all coinage and bills in circulation.

Demand deposit is the term used to describe the balances held in accounts in banks and institutions by the customers.

Reserve is the term used for the commercial bank's holdings of deposits in accounts with the central bank.

Fractional reserve banking is the banking practice in which only a fraction of a bank's demand deposits and currency are kept as reserves for withdrawal. The bank lends out most of the deposited funds, this is practiced by all modern commercial banks.

"The reserve ratio on net transactions accounts depends on the amount of net transactions accounts at the depository institution. The Garn-St Germain Act of 1982 exempted the first $2 million of reservable liabilities from reserve requirements. This "exemption amount" is adjusted each year according to a formula specified by the act. The amount of net transaction

accounts subject to a reserve requirement ratio of 3 percent was set under the Monetary Control Act of 1980 at $25 million. This "low-reserve tranche" is also adjusted each year (see table of low-reserve tranche amounts and exemption amounts since 1982). Net transaction accounts in excess of the low-reserve tranche are currently reservable at 10 percent."

Source:
http://www.federalreserve.gov/monetarypolicy/reserver eq.htm#table1

The excerpt from the Fed website above shows that reserves from 3 to 10 percent are imposed on the commercial banks depending on the amount of their demand deposits. What this means is that if you deposit $1000.00 dollars in your personal or business checking account your $1000.00 dollars is added to the money supply as a demand deposit. With a reserve set to 10% your bank in turn uses $900 dollars as loans to another client of the bank. This new client deposits his $900 dollars into his banking account increasing the money supply by $900 the bank can then loan $810 dollars to another client. Every time this process is performed it increases the money supply without printing any. The more money the commercial banks lend out the larger the money supply grows. The problem with this system is that if all the depositors came and demanded their money the bank would not be able to pay. The system relies on the concept that all the depositors will keep their money in the bank.

This is not the only problem in the expansion of the money supply. The most peculiar and hard to swallow function of the Federal Reserve Bank is the way it creates money. When the government needs money it issues IOU's called treasury securities. Like a certificate of deposit, it is a promise to pay the holder of the certificate a particular sum of money with accrued interest. These securities can be purchased by individual investors, pension funds, mutual funds, insurance agencies, commercial banks, foreign government's central banks, for the purpose of making money on their investments. Because the government has the power to collect taxes the treasury security is considered to be a safe investment. When a commercial bank buys the treasury bills they sell them to the Federal Reserve Bank who credits the amount to the commercial banks account at the Federal Reserve Bank in their district, in the amount of the Treasury bill and then holds the treasury bills as collateral. The amount is just credited into the commercial banks account by computer it does not come from any other source. There is no deposit made into the Federal Reserve Bank from anyplace "the buck starts here" should be their motto. To understand the absurdities of this imagine owning a checkbook that you could write checks for any amount of money to purchase as much as you wanted. With this account you never had to make a deposit. The stroke of an accountant's pen is all that is needed for the Federal Reserve Bank to create money from nothing. The member commercial bank then uses the money that is created in their account by the Federal Reserve Bank to loan to customers starting the fractional reserve banking system all over again. Then take this even further down the bizarre trail to understand that the federal government using your tax dollars is responsible to pay the interest on the treasury securities held by the Federal Reserve Banks that they bought using the magic checkbook.

When the supply of fiat money expands the prices on commodities will rise. It is kind of like a stock split only in reverse. When a publicly traded company doubles their shares the price of the stock is cut in half. If you had 1000 shares of stock valued at one dollar per share and the company issues a stock split you now own 2000 shares of stock at fifty cents. Because the company's assets are worth the same amount of money before and after the stock split doubling their stock doesn't make them worth double in hard assets. In simplistic terms when the Fed doubles the amount of money in circulation the price of the commodities you buy doubles because of the same basic principle. The larger the money supply the less the money will be worth.

Several historical observations of the central bank and our monetary policy since the inception of the Federal Reserve Act of 1913 must be settled to help us understand how America, from the beginning of the twentieth century, went from the greatest creditor nation in the world to the fourteen trillion dollar deficit nation that we are today.

The Federal Reserve manipulates the monetary policies of the US in three major ways;

1. It can buy or sell treasury securities.
2. Change the discount rate.
3. Adjust the reserve requirement.

For the first twenty five years the monetary policy of the Federal Reserve in regards to money creation was constrictive. In terms of interest rates they were kept artificially low to stimulate the growth that led to the stock market bubble. The events that dominated this era were the stock market crash, the massive bank failures and the great depression. Remember this is the monster that was created by the JP Morgan and Rockefeller "money trust" referred to in the previous chapters.

According to Ben Bernanke, the current Chairman of the Federal Reserve, the stock market crash and the subsequent depression were actually caused by tight monetary policies that the Federal Reserve instituted at that time.

Ben Bernanke highlighted several key Fed interventions:

- *The Fed began raising the Fed Funds rate in the spring of 1928, and kept raising it through a recession that began in August 1929. This led to the stock market crash in October 1929.*
- *When the stock market crashed, investors turned to the currency markets. At that time, dollars were backed by gold held by the U.S. Government. Speculators began selling dollars for gold in September 1931, which caused a run on the dollar.*
- *The Fed raised interest rates again to preserve the value of the dollar. This further restricted the availability of money for businesses, causing more bankruptcies.*
- *The Fed did not increase the supply of money to combat deflation.*
- *As investors withdrew all their dollars from banks, the banks failed, causing more panic. The Fed ignored the banks' plight, thus destroying any remaining consumers' confidence in banks. Most people withdrew their cash and put it under the mattress, which further decreased the money supply.*

Milton Freidman winner of the Nobel Prize in Economics was an Austrian school economist, a statistician, a professor at the University of Chicago, and economic advisor to U.S. President Ronald Reagan. In Freidman's book *A Monetary History of the United States* he demonstrated decisively that the monetary policies of the time were to blame for the Great Depression. At the celebration of Milton Friedman's 90th birthday in 2002 Ben Bernanke chairman of the Federal Reserve honored him with the words, "I would like to say to Milton and Anna: Regarding the Great Depression, you're right. We did it. We're very sorry." Friedman explains that the Federal Reserve was created to avert the very disaster that was the Great Depression. The Monetary policy of the era is ambiguous given the fact that if the Federal Reserve acted responsibly it could have easily stopped it from ever getting out of control. Friedman concluded that the Great Depression was not the result of the stock-market crash of October 1929, which he attribute to a speculative investment bubble exacerbated by the Federal Reserve's raising of the discount rate in August 1929 weeks before the crash. Friedman said the depression was due to the Fed's failure to be the lender of last resort just standing idly by as banks failed. Friedman wrote in Free to Choose:

"The [Federal Reserve] System could have provided a far better solution by engaging in large-scale open market purchases of government bonds. That would have provided banks with additional cash to meet the demands of their depositors. That would have ended— or at least sharply reduced—the stream of bank failures and have prevented the public's attempted conversion of deposits into currency from reducing the quantity of

money. Unfortunately, the Fed's actions were hesitant and small. In the main, it stood idly by and let the crisis take its course—a pattern of behavior that was to be repeated again and again during the next two years."

Matters were made worse when the free market economy was trashed by government intervention with policies that seem to defy commonsense. At the height of the depression the Federal Government passed the largest tax increase in the history of the country. Then they passed the Smoot-Hawley Tariff Act in 1930 decreasing demand for US exports eliminating factory jobs. Public works programs removed hundreds of thousands of people from the labor market making it harder for natural adjustment to the economy. The National Recovery Administration enacted policies that curtailed the creation of new business. The Federal Reserve increased bank-reserve requirements decreasing the money supply instead of increasing it to help the economy. Every time the economy showed signs of slight recovery the government and the fed enacted a policy to kill it.

In a bizarre turn of events in 1933 FDR Issued Presidential Order 6102 forcing all gold to be traded for Federal Reserve Paper. The penalty for resisting was $10,000 in fines and up to 10 years in prison. In the name of national emergency in banking the Fed was allowed to pillage the American public at gun point of all their gold for $20 an ounce. When the confiscation was complete FDR removed the Gold standard and within one year gold rose to $35 an ounce giving the Fed a 75% return on the gold. The actions of the Federal Reserve with the collusion of the US Government seamed to lead the world into the great depression and ultimately into World War II. The gold confiscation act is produced here in its entirety just in case you're having trouble believing it.

The Gold Confiscation of April 5, 1933
From: President of the United States Franklin Delano Roosevelt
To: The United States Congress
Dated: 5 April, 1933
Presidential Executive Order 6102

Forbidding the Hoarding of Gold Coin, Gold Bullion and Gold Certificates By virtue of the authority vested in me by Section 5(b) of the Act of October 6, 1917, as amended by Section 2 of the Act of March 9, 1933, entitled

An Act to provide relief in the existing national emergency in banking, and for other purposes~',

in which amendatory Act Congress declared that a serious emergency exists,

I, Franklin D. Roosevelt, President of the United States of America, do declare that said national emergency still continues to exist and pursuant to said section to do hereby prohibit the hoarding gold coin, gold bullion, and gold certificates within the continental United States by individuals, partnerships, associations and corporations and hereby prescribe the following regulations for carrying out the purposes of the order:

Section 1. For the purpose of this regulation, the term 'hoarding" means the withdrawal and withholding of gold coin, gold bullion, and gold certificates from the recognized and customary channels of trade. The term "person" means any individual, partnership, association or corporation.

Section 2. All persons are hereby required to deliver on or before May 1, 1933, to a Federal Reserve bank or a branch or agency thereof or to any member bank of the Federal Reserve System all gold coin, gold bullion, and gold certificates now owned by them or coming into their ownership on or before April 28, 1933, except the following:

(a) Such amount of gold as may be required for legitimate and customary use in industry, profession or art within a reasonable time, including gold prior to refining and stocks of gold in reasonable amounts for the usual trade requirements of owners mining and refining such gold.

(b) Gold coin and gold certificates in an amount not exceeding in the aggregate $100.00 belonging to any one person; and gold coins having recognized special value to collectors of rare and unusual coins.

(c) Gold coin and bullion earmarked or held in trust for a recognized foreign government or foreign central bank or the Bank for International Settlements.

(d) Gold coin and bullion licensed for the other proper transactions (not involving hoarding) including gold coin and gold bullion imported for the re-export or held pending action on applications for export license.

Section 3. Until otherwise ordered any person becoming the owner of any gold coin, gold bullion, and gold certificates after April 28, 1933, shall within three days after receipt thereof, deliver the same in the manner prescribed in Section 2; unless such gold coin, gold bullion, and gold certificates are held for any of the purposes specified in paragraphs (a),(b) or (c) of Section 2; or unless such gold coin, gold bullion is held for purposes specified in paragraph (d) of Section 2 and the person holding it is, with respect to such gold coin or bullion, a licensee or applicant for license pending action thereon.

Section 4. Upon receipt of gold coin, gold bullion, or gold certificates delivered to it in accordance with Section 2 or 3, the Federal reserve bank or member bank will pay thereof an equivalent amount of any other form of coin or currency coined or issued under the laws of the Unites States.

Section 5. Member banks shall deliver all gold coin, gold bullion, and gold certificates owned or received by them (other than as exempted under the provisions of Section 2) to the Federal reserve banks of their respective districts and receive credit or payment thereof.

Section 6. The Secretary of the Treasury, out of the sum made available to the President by Section 501 of the Act of March 9, 1933, will in all proper cases pay the reasonable costs of transportation of gold coin, gold bullion, and gold certificates delivered to a member bank or Federal reserve bank in accordance with Sections 2, 3, or 5 hereof, including the cost of insurance, protection, and such other incidental costs as may be necessary, upon production of satisfactory evidence of such costs. Voucher forms for this purpose may be procured from Federal reserve banks.

Section 7. In cases where the delivery of gold coin, gold bullion, or gold certificates by the owners thereof within the time set forth above will involve extraordinary hardship or difficulty, the Secretary of the Treasury may, in his discretion, extend the time within which such delivery must be made. Applications for such extensions must be made in writing under oath; addressed to the Secretary of the Treasury and filed with a Federal reserve bank. Each applications must state the date to which the extension is desired, the amount and location of the gold coin, gold bullion, and gold certificates in respect of which such application is made and the facts showing extension to be necessary to avoid extraordinary hardship or difficulty.

Section 8. The Secretary of the Treasury is hereby authorized and empowered to issue such further regulations as he may deem necessary to carry the purposes of this order and to issue licenses there under, through such officers or agencies as he may designate, including licenses permitting the Federal reserve banks and member banks of the Federal Reserve System, in return for an equivalent amount of other coin, currency or credit, to deliver, earmark or hold in trust gold coin or bullion to or for persons showing the need for same for any of the purposes specified in paragraphs (a), (c), and (d) of Section 2 of these regulations.

Section 9. Whoever willfully violates any provision of this Executive Order or these regulation or of any rule, regulation or license issued there under may be fined not more than $10,000, or,if a natural person may be imprisoned for not more than ten years or both; and any officer, director, or agent of any corporation who knowingly participates in any such violation may be punished by a like fine, imprisonment, or both.

This order and these regulations may be modified or revoked at any time.
Franklin D. Roosevelt
President of the United States of America
April 5, 1933

The only thing that took America out of the depression was World War II. The constrictive monetary policy of the previous era was finally lifted to prepare American industry for the war. Unemployment ended in the United States with the beginning of World War II. An increase in wartime production created millions of new jobs and the war pulled young men out of the workforce creating employment for women on factory floors. The race for military technical supremacy drove American industry and the federal government to a spending philosophy that would bring the US superpower status. New developments in aviation, shipping, weapons and communications spurred scientific research and development that would shape the world for the next fifty years. On an economic scale the war positively ended the great depression and in so doing brought together the federal government, private enterprise and labor to continue the economic growth caused by the war.

The U.S. surfaced from the war economically bolstered by wartime industrial growth, placing the United States above both its allies and its enemies. With this new found international power the United States Federal Reserve Bank would now be lender of last resort to the world bringing it one step closer to total global dominance. To solidify this power on the new system for international trade and finance they called for an international summit that became known as the Bretton wood conference. 730 delegates from all 44 Allied nations gathered at the Mount Washington Hotel in Bretton Woods, New Hampshire, for the United Nations Monetary and Financial Conference. The conference would be defined by plans prepared by two men, the British economist John Maynard Keynes and American Harry Dexter White, chief international economist at the U.S. Treasury. Keynes submitted a system that would use a world central bank that would be given the power to create money similar to the Federal Reserve by establishing a world reserve currency that he called the "bancor". Large international commercial banks would become members of the world central bank and operate on a global scale. This plan would have taken the sovereignty of the US and made America a slave to the world central bank.

White opposed Keynes plan and proposed his intention centered on the creation of the International Monetary Fund (IMF). The IMF would be no more than a fixed amount of national currencies and gold maintained by each country as opposed to a world central bank capable of creating money. The IMF would regulate trade deficits to oppose currency devaluations that produce declines in imports. Whites plan also called for the creation of the International Bank for Reconstruction and Development (IBRD) to promote the growth of world trade and to finance the postwar reconstruction of Europe. The US, eager to impose its overwhelming economic and military power and not wanting to relinquish control to a world central bank induced the participants at Bretton Woods to agree on White's plan.

Under the new Bretton Woods System the new international reserve currency became the US Dollar and formed the basis of the world's financial system. Because of the United States unique ability to print dollars it gave America an overwhelming advantage over other nations for trade financing. The US is the only country in the world that doesn't pay for its imports in a foreign currency. This advantage becomes a great disadvantage over time because of the massive amount of cash needed to finance world trade. This greatly amplified the money supply further boosting inflation.

The post war era of monetary policy can be attributed sadly to economist John Maynard Keynes. The early part of the post war era until the late seventies was dominated by the economic philosophies of Keynes and became known as Keynesian economics. Keynesian economics is considered the most influential economic doctrine guiding almost every government in the world. His major policy view was total government regulation. That the way to stabilize the economy is to stabilize the price level, and to do that the government's central bank must lower interest rates or raise them according to unemployment and inflation rates. This is the practice still used by the Federal Reserve today.

Keynes's theorized that full employment could be maintained only with the help of government spending. He believed government should fill the shoes of business by investing in public works and hiring the unemployed. His General Theory presented that deficit spending during economic downturns was the only way to maintain full employment.

He was opposed by those who believed in the Austrian school of economics such as Carl Menger, Friedrich Hayek, Ludwig Von Mises, Murray Rothbard and Milton Freidman. The Austrian school of economics maintains that the ecomomy is better served without any government intervention in a decentralized free market economy. That the economy is regulated naturally by supply and demand.

Keynes's ideology of deficit spending soon permeated into the halls of Washington and once policymakers began to use it they couldn't stop. Keynesian economics through the fifties and sixties produced a false sense of prosperity built on debt and inflation. President Nixon once claimed, "We are all Keynesians now."

Deficit spending is the spending practice by which a government, private company, or individual's purchasing exceeds income. The opposite of deficit spending is **sound finance** which rejects Keynesianism in favor of a balanced budget. Sound finance advocates producing a surplus to pay down any outstanding debt and that deficit spending is bad policy. Debts must be repaid, which burdens future generations who will be required to pay increased taxes in the future, debts that did not produce any benefit for them. Milton Friedman argued that government deficits are inflationary. Any inflation is generally accepted in economics to be a bad thing because governments pay off debts by printing more fiat money, increasing the money supply which then causes more inflation leading to more debt.

The Keynesian economic model took a severe blow in the seventies with the advent of stagflation. This is a difficult economic condition where inflation and unemployment were consistently and dangerously high. Keynes philosophy could not be used to control stagflation because his one method of governing the economy by raising or lowering interest rates was flawed. When this occurs the central bank is in a difficult position in regards to interest rates, raising the interest rates lead to even higher unemployment while lowering the interest rates lead to higher inflation. This conflicted with the basic principle of Keynes economic philosophy of control and his failure is our exact predicament today.

In an effort to return to fiscal responsibility President Ronald Reagan adopted a conservative financial agenda that outlined four basic principles of his administration; Reduce government spending, Reduce income and capital gains marginal tax rates, Reduce government regulation and Control the money supply to reduce inflation. Present Reagan in 1981 passed the economic recovery tax act which greatly reduced revenues to the federal government. Due to the drastic cuts in upper income brackets this ideology became known as "trickle down economics". Reagan's tax cuts deregulation and conservative monetary policy created an economic expansion giving America a sustained wave of prosperity. The economy expanded by more than thirty percent. Most Americans saw an increase in their incomes during Reagan's term in office. To those who see the expansion of wealth during the Reagan years as a return to the conservative principles that produced prosperity in the 19th century they need only look at the impact Reaganomics had on the national debt which rose from \$997 billion to \$2.85 trillion according to the US treasury department. This massive increase of 286 percent moved the United States from being the world's largest international creditor to the world's largest debtor nation.

The present phase of the US monetary policy has been headed by Alan Greenspan Chairman of the board of governors since 1987. Appointed by Ronald Reagan he was reappointed by Bill Clinton and George W. Bush and held the position until 2006 when he was replaced by Ben Bernanke. He presided over the Federal Reserve during the 1987 Stock market crash, the 1991 recession, the tech boom of the 90's, the pop of the dot com bubble in 2000 and the housing crises of 2006. During his tenure the national debt rose from 2.85 to 8.2 trillion. During this time America endured two wars in Iraq and one in Afghanistan along with countless actions of foreign intervention with UN security forces around the world and the attacks of 9/11. We witnessed the collapse of Enron, Lehman Bros., AIG, Freddie Mac and Fannie Mae, Merrill Lynch, bankruptcy of General Motors and the collapse of the US housing bubble. Beginning in 2008 The U.S. Federal Reserve and central banks around the world have taken steps to expand money supplies to combat unemployment and lower wages leading to a spiraling decline in global consumption.

From 2000 to 2007 The United States was responsible for thirty percent of the world's consumption until the 2008 meltdown of the US economy caused downturns in countries around the globe. Since then governments have enacted large fiscal stimulus packages, borrowing and spending to offset the reduction in private sector demand caused by the crisis. This has raised the national debt to 14 trillion dollars reaching nearly 100 percent of the Gross Domestic Product. What does this mean for the future of the United States? How much debt burden can be shouldered by the people of America before a total collapse of our society?

After World War I Germany was forced to accept and sign the Treaty of Versailles which contained agreements that Germany was to pay all war reparations over time. The debt of the war coupled with the war reparations made Germany's national debt to foreign interests over 100 percent of the nation's gross domestic product. The German government began printing money to pay the massive debt but as it increased the money supply inflation lead to hyperinflation and in two years the German mark plummeted from 4.2 per US Dollar before World War I to 4.2 trillion to 1 US Dollar in December of 1923. The German people were using their bank notes to paper their walls. The economic depression in Germany gave rise to the Nazi war machine and Hitler.

What happens when the US debt exceeds America's ability to shoulder the interest payments? Do we keep printing money as Germany did in 1922? Another thing you have to take into consideration is that the German Mark was not the foundational currency of the world's economy like the US Dollar is today. If the Dollar fails due to the Federal Reserve's "quantitative easing" practices, hyperinflation will affect every country in the world.

Declining Value of the US Dollar (USD)

On March 18, 2009 The New York Times ran the following article:

*"WASHINGTON — The Federal Reserve sharply stepped up its efforts to bolster the economy on Wednesday, announcing that it would pump an extra $1 trillion into the financial system by purchasing Treasury bonds and mortgage securities. Having already reduced the key interest rate it controls nearly to zero, the central bank has increasingly turned to alternatives like buying securities as a way of getting more dollars into the economy, **a tactic that amounts to creating vast new sums of money out of thin air**. But the moves on Wednesday were its biggest yet, almost doubling all of the Fed's measures in the last year. ...But there were also **clear indications that the Fed was taking risks that could dilute the value of the dollar and set the stage for future inflation.** Gold prices rose $26.60 an ounce, hitting $942, a sign of declining confidence in the dollar. The dollar, which*

had been losing value in recent weeks to the euro and the yen, dropped sharply again on Wednesday...."

The Times states that the Federal Reserve is creating vast new sums of money out of thin air to help the economy. This has clear indications that these actions lead to the dilution of our currency as gold prices rise sharply proving that inflation is a direct result of the expanded money supply. From 2000 to 2010 the American people have paid over four trillion dollars in interest alone on the US Government treasury securities. The question is what is the collateral that is being used for the United States Federal debt of fourteen trillion dollars? The entire US reserve of gold is only approximately four hundred billion, that's not enough to cover three percent of the national debt or barely enough to cover the interest for one year. The collateral is you, the American people and when that is not enough it will be our children and grand children. As Thomas Jefferson said, *"If the people ever allow the banks to issue their currency, the banks and corporations which will grow up around them will deprive the people of all property, until their children wake up homeless on the continent their fathers conquered."* These prophetic words haunt us today as our leaders succumb to the plans of the Federal Reserve and its wise board of Governors who in the name of helping the American people have robbed us of everything.

Inflation is at an all time high and has risen consistently throughout the century. American families are finding it more difficult to make ends meet. Unemployment has passed ten percent, home sales are down to their lowest levels and home repossessions are being performed at an alarming rate. Small business and personal bankruptcies have become the norm. If the Federal Reserve Act was created to control economic challenges they have proved utter failure in that respect and have no clue as to what moves markets in any direction. Why have the actions of the Federal Reserve proved so imprudent, dangerous and reckless to our economy and country? To this there are only two scenarios, on the one hand is the idea that the all the university educated economist and financial analysts since 1913 who have assisted the Federal Reserve Board of Governors on monetary policies for the benefit of the American people and the success of the economy have been at their very best incompetent. On the other hand is the idea that **the goals of the Federal Reserve are not for the benefit of the American people and the success of the economy but lie in the schemes of those private banks who own the Federal Reserve**.

In the span of approximately eleven months February 3, 1913 to December 23, 1913 three treacherous acts of treason were perpetrated by the same cabal of power hungry men that were defendants in the Pujo Committee in the "Money Trust" investigation. These acts were the Sixteenth Amendment, the Seventeenth Amendment and the Federal Reserve Act. Three villainous acts created in unison to enslave the American public. The income tax Sixteenth Amendment is used to pay the interest to the Federal Reserve while the Seventeenth Amendment removed the checks and balances of the states to oppose the federal governments new found power. To recap since the Federal Reserve was created it was responsible for the Stock market crash of 1929, The Great Depression, the confiscation of all the gold, made its currency the global monetary unit used for trade around the world, put us in more debt that we can pay and has charted a course for the American economy that will only lead to the nations demise and finally to a fascist state controlled by the "money trust gods".

Chapter 7

"Globalization"

The term "globalization" has become the catch phrase for the 21st century. It alludes to a natural process that is affecting the world through economics, communication, society, culture, trade, foreign policy, environment and military intervention. The term would lead you to believe that somehow no matter what the controls of society and humanity propagate that the world is on a collision course to become one global society controlled by a set of rules that no one actually created but were collectively produced by some sort of accidental evolution of human connectivity.

Globalization is not a natural occurrence it has been scientifically planned and meticulously nurtured and its course is being perpetually navigated by elite world powers through foreign policy. The first major modern day attempt to collectively bring people from other countries together for world unification was the formation of the League of Nations after World War I. About the same time the "money trust" formed the Federal Reserve they were already turning their attention to globalization. With the "war to end all wars" over, President Woodrow Wilson, looking for solutions to all the postwar problems of the world, commissioned his advisor Colonel Edward M. House to head an inquiry of one hundred and fifty academic experts to frame capable solutions and a constitution for the League of Nations. House aided in the creation of Wilsons Fourteen Points and the details of the armistice with the Allies and the drafting of the Treaty of Versailles. The League of Nations was established, but it and the plan for world government eventually failed because the U.S. Senate would not ratify the Versailles Treaty.

"On May 30, 1919 at a dinner meeting at the Majestic Hotel in Paris conversations between Gen Tasker H. Bliss, Col. E. M. House, Prof. Archibald Cary Coolidge, Whitney H. Shepardson, Dr. James T. Shotwell and others of the American delegation, and British officials such as Sir Robert Cecil, Lionel Curtis, Sir Valentine Chirol, Lord Eustace Percy and Harold Temperley formally agreed that an organization should be created for the study of international affairs. The first two resolutions set forth the proposed form and substance of the undertaking: 'RESOLVED: That those present undertake to form an Institute entitled The Institute of International Affairs. Founded in Paris in 1919 comprised at the outset of two branches, one in the United Kingdom and one in the U.S." Emanuel Josephson, Rockefeller "Internationalist" - NY: Chedney Press, 1952 pp. 237-38.

At this meeting in Paris was laid the groundwork for the establishment of an intellectual college of academics. The attendees would select men, only of their choosing, to become members, directors, presidents and vice presidents of a school of thought. The major goal was to indoctrinate the public at large of the needs for global solutions in government, economics and environment. This became known as the Council on Foreign Relations in the US and its British counterpart the Institute of Foreign Affairs at the Chatham House in London. Founded in 1921 and headquartered at 58 East 68th Street in New York City, with an additional office in Washington, D.C., the CFR became to be considered the nation's most influential foreign-policy think tank. The CFR Website claims its mission to be:

"a resource for its members, government officials, business executives, journalists, educators and students, civic and religious leaders, and other interested citizens in order to help them better understand the world and the foreign policy choices facing the United States and other countries."

The visual aim of this organization is undeniably globalist the hidden agenda is far more sinister. From its inception it was and still remains a private foundation and has no formal ties to the government. The citizens of the United States have absolutely no influence to what they teach or publish; membership is highly exclusive and can only be obtained by invitation and sponsorship of current membership. At first it was formed to accomplish the provisions previously outlined in the League of Nations. The makeup of a General Assembly, Executive Council and a permanent secretariat, member nations expected to "respect and preserve as against external aggression" the territorial integrity of other nations, disarmament "to the lowest point consistent with domestic safety" and a World Court of International Justice. Over the course of its ninety year history it has transformed itself into the most indoctrinating power of globalism in the world today and the protector of the United Nations. The following testimony before the US Senate by James Warburg CFR Member and son of Paul M. Warburg one of the original founders of the Federal Reserve reveals the global nature of the organization. (Not printed in entirety due to space.)

February 17, 1950
Washington, D. C.
REVISION OF THE UNITED NATIONS CHARTER

Hearings before a Subcommittee of the Committee on
Foreign Relations
United States Senate
81st Congress, 2d Session
on Resolutions relative to the United Nations charter,
Atlantic Union, World Federation, etc.
Feb. 2, 3, 6, 8, 9, 13, 15, 17, and 20, 1950
Printed for the use of the Committee on Foreign Relations
U.S. GOVERNMENT PRINTING OFFICE,
WASHINGTON, 1950: 64429
PP. 494-508

Subcommittee on Revision of the United Nations
Charter
Elbert D. Thomas, Utah, Chairman
Theodor Francis Green, Rhode Island
Alexander Wiley, Wisconsin
H. Alexander Smith, New Jersey

I am James P. Warburg, of Greenwich, Conn.,
and am appearing as an individual.

I am aware, Mr. Chairman, of the exigencies
of your crowded schedule and of the need to
be brief, so as not to transgress upon your
courtesy in granting me a hearing.

The past 15 years of my life have been
devoted almost exclusively to studying the
problem of world peace and, especially, the
relation of the United States to these

problems. These studies led me, 10 years ago, to the conclusion that the great question of our time is not whether or not one world can be achieved, but whether or not one world can be achieved by peaceful means.

We shall have world government, whether or not we like it. The question is only whether world government will be achieved by consent or by conquest…..

… Mr. Chairman, I am here to testify in favor of Senate Resolution 56, which, if concurrently enacted with the House, would make the peaceful transformation of the United Nations into a world federation the avowed aim of United States policy. The passage of this resolution seems to me the first prerequisite toward the development of an affirmative American policy which would lead us out of the valley of death and despair.

First: Senate Resolution 56 goes to the root of the evil in the present state of international anarchy. It recognizes that there is no cure for this evil short of making the United Nations into a universal organization capable of enacting, interpreting, and enforcing world law to the degree necessary to outlaw force, or the threat of force, as an instrument of foreign policy. It states the objective in unequivocal terms.

"The best way to fight Communism is by a One World socialist state governed by experts like themselves. The result has been policies which favor, gradual surrender of United States sovereignty to the United Nations."
- Granddaughter of Theodore Roosevelt, Edith Kermit

Roosevelt, writing about the CFR point of view in the *Indianapolis News*, Dec. 23, 1961

With its biweekly publication Foreign Affairs, frequent discussion groups, daily news briefs, debates, books, lectures, seminars, task force and special council reports members are influenced to believe that the only way to peace and prosperity is to form the global community. The creators and directors of the CFR unanimously desire a universal government. The most alarming thing about this group is that its leaders and directors have always been among the most powerful and influential people of their time. Membership has grown to approximately 4300 persons among them are scientist, environmentalists, journalist, media moguls, directors of multinational corporations, presidential cabinet members, economist, federal reserve bankers, ambassadors, actors, directors, news anchors, US intelligence officers, and the list continues. Most members believe in what they are doing and are incognizant of the truth that this organization is created as a means to a perpetrated end. As for the leaders of this organization the motives are much more complicated and individually diverse with varying levels of involvement and passion according to their economic status and power. To further its aims the CFR has cross memberships to similar institutions, all with the same agenda.

The Trilateral Commission - a private organization, established to foster closer cooperation among the United States, Europe and Japan. It was founded in July 1973 at the initiative of David Rockefeller, who was Chairman of the Council on Foreign Relations at that time. The Trilateral Commission is widely seen as an off-shoot of the Council on Foreign Relations. Speaking at the Chase Manhattan International Financial Forums in London, Brussels, Montreal, and Paris, Rockefeller proposed the creation of an International Commission of Peace and Prosperity in early 1972. Funding for the group came from David Rockefeller, the Charles F. Kettering Foundation, and the Ford Foundation.

The group was organized by United States National Security Advisor to President Jimmy Carter from 1977 to 1981 Zbigniew Brzezinski other founding members included:

- Henry D. Owen (a Foreign Policy Studies Director with the Brookings Institution)
- George S. Franklin
- Robert R. Bowie (of the Foreign Policy Association and Director of the Harvard Center for International Affairs)
- Gerard C. Smith (Salt I negotiator, Rockefeller in-law, and its first North American Chairman)
- Marshall Hornblower (former partner at Wilmer, Cutler & Pickering)
- William Scranton (former Governor of Pennsylvania)
- Edwin Reischauer (a professor at Harvard)
- Max Kohnstamm (European Policy Centre)
- Alan Greenspan and Paul Volcker, both eventually head of the <u>Federal Reserve System</u>.

Current Leadership

- **North America:** Joseph S. Nye, Jr., University Distinguished Service Professor and former

Dean, John F. Kennedy School of Government, Harvard University, Cambridge, MA; former Chair, National Intelligence Council and former U.S. Assistant Secretary of Defense for International Security Affairs.

- **Europe Chairman:** Mario Monti President, Bocconi University, Milan; Member of the EU Reflection Group on the Future of Europe (Horizon 2020-2030); former Member of the European Commission (Competition Policy and Internal Market); Honorary President, BRUEGEL, Brussels
- **Pacific Asia:** Yotaro Kobayashi, Chief Corporate Adviser, Fuji Xerox Company, Ltd.; Board member of Callaway Golf Company, Nippon Telegraph and Telephone Corporation (NTT), Sony Corporation, and American Productivity & Quality Center; life-time trustee of Keizai Doyukai (Japan Association of Corporate Executives); Chairman of the Aspen Institute, Japan.

Membership stands at approximately 600 worldwide and is by invitation only, as the CFR membership is only extended to US citizens the Trilateral commission is extended globally.

Senator Barry Goldwater wrote in his book With No Apologies: *"In my view, the Trilateral Commission represents a skillful, coordinated effort to seize control and consolidate the four centers of power: political, monetary, intellectual, and ecclesiastical. All this is to be done in the interest of creating a more peaceful, more productive world community. What the Trilateralists truly intend is the creation of a worldwide economic power superior to the political governments of the nation-states involved. They believe the abundant materialism they propose to create will overwhelm existing differences. As managers and creators of the system they will rule the future."*

Carnegie Endowment for International Peace - Founded in 1910 by Andrew Carnegie as a foreign-policy think tank based in Washington, D.C. The organization describes itself as being dedicated to advancing cooperation between nations and promoting active international engagement by the United States. Like other leading internationalists of his day, Carnegie believed that war could be eliminated by stronger international laws and organizations. "*I am drawn more to this cause than to any*" he wrote in 1907. Andrew Carnegie announced the establishment of the Endowment with a gift of $10 million.

Stated in a book by Edmund Jan Osmanczyk, Anthony Mango (February 2004). *Encyclopedia of the United Nations and International Agreements*. Routledge ;.

"In his deed of gift, presented in Washington on December 14, 1910, Carnegie charged trustees to use the fund to "hasten the abolition of international war, the foulest blot upon our civilization," and he gave his trustees "the widest discretion as to the measures and policy they shall from time to time adopt" in carrying out the purpose of the fund.""

Carnegie chose longtime adviser and internationalist Elihu Root, the founding chairman of the Council on Foreign Relations, Senator from New York and former Secretary of War and of State, to be the Endowment's first president. Root supported the League of Nations and served on the commission of jurists, which created the Permanent Court of International Justice.

Original Trustees of the Carnegie Foundation:

- Charles William Eliot - Harvard University president
- Robert S. Brookings - philanthropist and founder of the Brookings Institute
- Joseph Hodges Choate - former U.S. Ambassador to Great Britain
- John W. Foster - former Secretary of State
- Henry Smith Pritchett - Carnegie Foundation for the Advancement of Teaching president

The Carnegie Endowment for International Peace is based out of several countries. In 1993, the Endowment launched the Carnegie Moscow Center, with the belief that, "*in today's world a think tank whose mission is to contribute to global security, stability, and prosperity requires a permanent presence and a multinational outlook at the core of its operations*". Carnegie's stated goal is to become the first multinational/global think tank. The Carnegie Endowment now has operations in several countries, with headquarters in Moscow, Beijing, Beirut, Brussels, and Washington, D.C.

Norman Dodd was chief investigator in 1953 for U.S. Congressman B. Carroll Reece on a Special Committee for Tax Exempt Foundations (commonly referred to as the Reece Committee). Mr. Dodd was given the handwritten minutes of the Foundation from its inception (1908 to 1953). The Dodd report is a document of his findings. In a video interview in 1984 he exposes the real agenda of all these institutions. It is called Norman Dodd on Tax Exempt Foundations. After viewing this hair raising interview your life may never be the same again.

The Brookings Institute – Founded by Robert Brookings one of the original trustees of the Carnegie Foundation for International peace. He was a friend of President Woodrow Wilson who appointed him to the War Industries Board. Wilson later named him chairman of the Price Fixing Committee, as a nonprofit public policy organization to conduct research and education in the social sciences. The sciences studied were primarily in economics, metropolitan policy, governance, foreign policy, and global economy. The committee was funded by an endowment from the Carnegie Foundation. In 1952, Robert Calkins president of the Brookings Institution secured grants from the Rockefeller Foundation and the Ford Foundation reorganizing the Institution around the Economic Studies, Government Studies, and Foreign Policy Programs.

Open Society Institute – Founded by CFR member and director George Soros the organization boasts they support justice, human rights, freedom of expression, public health, and education in more than 70 countries.

Some organizations that have received support from OSI:

Center for American Progress
Tides Foundation
Campaign for America's Future
National Council of La Raza

ACORN
Apollo Alliance
Center for Community Change
Free Press
MoveOn.org

In Soros book "The Crisis of Global Capitalism" he wrote, *"To stabilize and regulate a truly global economy, we need some global system of political decision-making. In short, we need a global society to support our global economy. A global society does not mean a global state. To abolish the existence of states is neither feasible nor desirable; but insofar as there are collective interests that transcend state boundaries,* ***the sovereignty of states must be subordinated to international law and international institutions.***"

He stated in an interview *"... when you try to improve society you affect different people and different interests differently and they are not actually commensurate, so you very often have all kinds of unintended adverse consequences, so I had to experiment. And it was a learning process. The first part was this subversive activity disrupting repressive regimes, that was a lot of fun and that was what actually got me hooked on the enterprise.... Seeing what works in one country so trying it in the other countries it was like what developed a matrix in fact you had national foundation and then we had certain actualized activities...* ***I became concerned with the problems of globalization where you have global markets but you have politics based on the sovereignty of states so how do you deal with that issue. And then I came to the realization that open society is endangered by our current leadership in this country*** *and then that is when I refocused my attention on the United States."*

George Soros is calling for all nations to subordinate themselves to a global international set of laws that would transcend the sovereignty of their state. This trend of global dominance is being purposely delivered by billions of dollars of scientifically administered institutionalism. It is designed to be driven towards our society and to be absorbed into the very fabric of America. The end game is to ultimately remove every freedom given to us by the Constitution and Bill of Rights.

The CFR, Trilateral Commission, Carnegie Endowment for International Peace, the Brookings Institute and the Open Society Institute have all been funded and perpetrated by those who all drink form the trough of globalism and world government. Their far reaching power and resources cannot be opposed without a grass roots effort of counter-education in truth. The American people must produce a broad based awaking to see that our way of life is in serious threat. This effort cannot be expected to come from our political leaders. We cannot trust our leaders to stop the onslaught because the foreign policy institutes have totally permeated the thinking in Washington. The small percentage of capable politicians are grossly outnumbered and perpetually frustrated by their fellow politicians who have conceded their ideology to the pressures of the internationalist. If you are unsure of the ability of these organizations to wield such influence over our lives you only have to see the rosters of their directors, leaders and members over the history of their organizations. For the last ninety years the policies of the US Government have been shaped by the ideology of these institutions. The insertions and appointments of their members to high level cabinet positions have influenced government policy makers and Presidents.

*"Such traitors will probably **endeavour first to get their prince into their possession**, and, like Sejanus, shut him up in a little island, or perhaps make him a prisoner in his court; whilst, with full range, they devour his dominions, and plunder his subjects. **When he is thus secluded from the access of his friends, and the knowledge of his affairs, he must be content with such misrepresentations as they shall find expedient to give him. False cases will be stated, to justify wicked counsel; wicked counsel will be given, to procure unjust orders.** He will be made to mistake his foes for his friends, his friends for his foes; and to believe that his affairs are in the highest prosperity, when they are in the greatest distress; and that publick matters go on in the greatest harmony, when they are in the utmost confusion.*

Cato's Letter No. 17
John Trenchard (February 18, 1721)

Currently President Obama's cabinet is heavily weighted with members of the CFR including; Secretary of the Treasury Timothy F. Geithner, Secretary of Defense Robert M. Gates, Secretary of Veteran Affairs Eric Shinseki, Secretary of Homeland Security Janet A. Napolitano, Whitehouse Chief of Staff William Daley, Director of the office of the management of the budget Jacob J. Lew, Ambassador to the UN Susan Rice. Listed are some of the most influential leaders of the CFR past and present to help you understand just how powerful this private organization has been and why the ideology of globalism is gaining dominance today.

Archibald Cary Coolidge – CFR Director (1921-28) One of the original dinner guests at the Paris meeting at the Majestic Hotel where the CFR was born. Professor of History at Harvard College from 1908, Director of the Harvard University Library from 1910 until his death.

Whitney H. Shepardson - CFR Director, Treasurer (1921-66) One of the original dinner guests at the Paris meeting at the Majestic Hotel where the CFR was born. A Rhodes Scholar, He headed the Secret Intelligence Branch of the Office of Strategic Services during World War II, director on John D. Rockefeller's General Education Board, director of the Woodrow Wilson Foundation. President of Bates International Bag Company, vice-president of International Railways of Central America, a transport arm of the United Fruit Company, in London, he was special assistant to the U.S. ambassador, and became first London head of Secret Intelligence, became head of the agency's Secret Intelligence Branch which would ultimately become part of the Central Intelligence Agency until 1946, president of the National Committee for a Free Europe.

David F. Houston - CFR Director (1921-27) US Secretary of the Treasury 1920-21 US Secretary of Agriculture 1913-1920 President of Bell Telephone Securities and a vice president at AT&T. Director AT&T, the Guaranty Trust Company and the United States Steel Corporation. He was president of the Mutual Life Insurance Company of New York for 10 years.

Edwin F. Gay - CFR Director, Secretary, Treasurer, Vice President (1921-45) He was the first dean of the Harvard Business School from 1908-1919. He was president of the New York Evening Post from 1920-1923.

John H. Finley - CFR Director (1921-29) appointed The New York Times associate editor in 1921. On April 21, 1937, The Times announced Dr. Finley's appointment as editor-in-chief. He held that position until Nov. 16, 1938.

John W. Davis - CFR Director (1921-55) United States Representative from West Virginia (1911–1913), then as Solicitor General of the United States and U.S. Ambassador to the UK under President Woodrow Wilson. Over a 60-year legal career, he argued 140 cases before the U.S. Supreme Court. Democratic Party nominee for President of the United States during the 1924 presidential election.

Otto H. Kahn - CFR Director (1921-34) Kuhn, Loeb & Co. in New York City Partner. Other partners included Jacob Schiff son-in-law of founder Solomon Loeb, and Paul and Felix Warburg. Director in numerous corporations, including the Equitable Trust Co. of New York and the Union Pacific railway

Frank L. Polk - CFR Director, Vice President (1921-43) Polk served on a variety of New York City boards and commissions. He served in the United States Department of State as Counselor (1915–1919), Acting Secretary of State (1920), and Under Secretary of State (1919–1920) American Commission to Negotiate Peace (1919)

Isaiah Bowman - CFR Director, Vice President (1921-50) director of the American Geographical Society, a position he held for 20 years from 1915 to 1935. He was chief territorial adviser to President Woodrow Wilson at the Versailles conference and served the Department of State as territorial adviser during World War II

Norman H. Davis - CFR Director, Vice President, President (1921-44) served as President Wilson's Assistant Secretary of Treasury and later as Undersecretary of State. He was a delegate to a General Disarmament Conference in Geneva in 1931. He was chairman of the International Federation of Red Cross and Red Crescent Societies from 1938 to 1944 and president of the Council on Foreign Relations 1936-1944. In 1939, following the outbreak of war in Europe, Davis chaired the steering committee of the Council on Foreign Relations' War and Peace Studies project, created to advise the U.S. Government on wartime policy

Paul M. Warburg - CFR Director (1921-32) Original founder of the Federal Reserve Bank and attendee of the infamous Jeckyl Island retreat and first President of the CFR and original member of the first Federal Reserve Board, chairman of the International Acceptance Bank of New York, Bank of the Manhattan Company, and Wels Fargo. Married Nina J. Loeb, daughter of Solomon Loeb, founder of Kuhn, Loeb & Company

Paul D. Cravath - CFR Director, Vice President (1921-40) Manhattan lawyer and a partner of the law firm today known as Cravath, Swaine & Moore

Stephen P. Duggan - CFR Director (1921-50) professor of diplomatic history at the College of the City of New York founded The Institute of International Education in 1919, together with Nobel Laureates Elihu Root and Nicholas Murray Butler

George O. May - CFR Director, Vice President (1927-53) States Treasury Department and the War Trade Board. President (1926-27) and chairman of the Board (1928-29) of the National Bureau of Economic Research; vice president, American Economic Association (1930); and director, American Statistical Association (1937-40)

Allen W. Dulles - CFR Director, Secretary, Vice President, President (1927-50) first Director of Central Intelligence, member of the Warren Commission, corporate lawyer and partner at Sullivan & Cromwell, directors of the J. Henry Schroder bank. His brother was the Secretary of State John Foster Dulles.

Owen D. Young - CFR Director (1927-40) member of the German Reparations International Commission. Founder of the Radio Corporation of America (RCA), GE's president and chairman, helped found the National Broadcasting Company (NBC). board of trustees of the Rockefeller Foundation. Young's participation in President Woodrow Wilson's Second Industrial Conference following World War I marked the beginning of his counseling of five U.S. presidents, Time Magazine's Man of the Year in 1929

Russell C. Leffingwell - CFR Director, Chairman, Vice President, President (1927-60) JP Morgan associate joined JP Morgan & Company in 1923, and he retired as chairman of the company in 1950

Walter H. Mallory - CFR Director, Executive Director (1927-68) On September 12, 1939, the Council on Foreign Relations began to take control of the Department of State. On that day Hamilton Fish Armstrong, Editor of Foreign Affairs, and Walter H. Mallory, Executive Director of the CFR, paid a visit to the State Department. The Council proposed forming groups of experts to proceed with research in the general areas of Security, Armament, Economic, Political, and Territorial problems. The State Department accepted the proposal. The project (1939-1945) was called "Council on Foreign Relations War and Peace Studies". Hamilton Fish Armstrong was Executive Director.

Elihu Root - CFR Honorary President (1931-37) attorney, US Senator NY 1909-15, US Secretary of War 1899-1904, US Secretary of State 1905-09 Root also had private clients including Jay Gould, Chester A. Arthur, Charles Anderson Dana, William C. Whitney, Thomas Fortune Ryan, and E. H. Harriman. Root was appointed U.S. Attorney for the Southern District of New York by President Chester A. Arthur.

Walter Lippmann - CFR Director (1932-37) adviser to President Woodrow Wilson and assisted in the drafting of Wilson's Fourteen Points speech, a journalist, a media critic and a philosopher, twice awarded (1958 and 1962) a Pulitzer Prize for his syndicated newspaper column, "Today and Tomorrow"

Clarence M. Woolley - CFR Director (1932-35) with the financing help of JP Morgan, Woolley's American Radiator revenue had reached a level of $100 million.

Frank Altschul - CFR Director, Secretary, Vice President, (1934-72) chairman of the board of the General American Investors Company, Inc

Philip C. Jessup - CFR Director (1934-42) assistant secretary-general of the United Nations, United Nations Monetary and Financial Conference (the "Bretton Woods" conference) in 1944. He was a technical advisor to the American delegation to the San Francisco United Nations charter conference in 1945, U.S. candidate for the International Court of Justice

Harold W. Dodds - CFR Director (1935-43) President of Princeton

Leon Fraser - CFR Director (1936-45) President of The First National Bank of the City of New York, appeared before the Committee on Banking and Currency of the House of Representatives to testify on the Bretton Woods Agreement Act, President of the world bank for international settlements. The second BIS president in the first two years of Hitler's assumption of power, influential in financing the Nazis through the BIS

Lewis W. Douglas - CFR Director (1940-64) US Ambassador to the United Kingdom, Director of the bureau of the budget, US House of Representatives for AZ

Henry M. Wriston - CFR Director, Vice President. President (1943-67) President of the American Assembly and Board of Trustees of the World Peace Foundation, adviser to President Eisenhower, a member of the United States Department of State's Advisory Committee on Foreign Service, Chairman of the Historical Advisory Committee to the Chief of Military History for the United States Department of the Army, father of Walter Wriston, former chairman and CEO of Citibank

Myron C. Taylor - CFR Director (1943-59) associate of J.P. Morgan and George F. Baker U.S. Steel's chairman and chief executive officer

Thomas K. Finletter - CFR Director (1944-67) special assistant to Secretary of State Cordell Hull on international economic affairs, executive director and later deputy director of the Office of Foreign Economic Coordinator (OFEC), consultant at the United Nations Conference on International Organization at San Francisco, cosigner of the "Declaration of the Dublin, N.H., Conference", a declaration on world peace issued by the Dublin Conference on World Peace. The declaration stated that the United Nations was inadequate to maintain world peace, and advocated a world federal government, appointed by President Harry S. Truman to form a committee that became known as the "The Finletter Commission", Secretary of the Air Force succeeding, Ambassador to NATO

Winfield W. Riefler - CFR Director (1945-50) Federal Reserve Economist and one of the founders of the United Nations

Philip D. Reed - CFR Director (1945-69) Reed joined GE in 1927, and became President and CEO in 1940, during the Second World War worked for the War Production Board and later with the U.S. Mission for Economic Affairs, eventually succeeding Averell Harriman as head of the USMEA office in London when Harriman was appointed U.S. Ambassador to the Soviet Union

William A. M. Burden - CFR Director (1945-74) Heir to the Vanderbilt fortune

David Rockefeller – CFR Director, Vice President, Chairman (1949-85) patriarch of the Rockefeller family. He is the youngest child of John D. Rockefeller, Jr. and Abby Aldrich Rockefeller, and the grandchild of oil tycoon John D. Rockefeller, founder of Standard Oil

Joseph E. Johnson - CFR Director (1950-74) served with both the United States Department of State and the United Nations

Grayson Kirk - CFR Director, Vice Chairman, President (1950-73) professor University of Wisconsin–Madison, Associate Professor of Government at Columbia, During World War II began a long association with the U.S. Federal Government when he served in the Security Section of the Department of State's Political Studies Division, involved in the formation of the United Nations Security Council, attending the Dumbarton Oaks Conference and the United Nations Conference on International Organization where the United Nations Charter was signed

W. Averell Harriman - CFR Director (1950-55) son of railroad baron E. H. Harriman, Secretary of Commerce under President Harry S. Truman and later as the 48th Governor of New York, candidate for the Democratic Presidential Nomination in 1952, and again in 1956 when he was endorsed by President Truman but lost to Adlai Stevenson, served President Franklin D. Roosevelt as special envoy to Europe, U.S. Ambassador to the Soviet Union, U.S. Ambassador to Britain, served in various positions in the Kennedy and Johnson administrations

Devereux C. Josephs - CFR Director, Treasurer, Vice President (1951-58) board of directors Morgan Guaranty Trust Company

Elliott V. Bell - CFR Director, Treasurer (1953-66) Chairman, executive committee, McGraw-Hill, editor and publisher, Business Week, superintendent of banking, New York State, editorial board The New York Times, writer and assistant financial editor, The New York Times financial writer, banking and money-market specialist, The New York Herald Tribune

George S. Franklin, Jr. - CFR Executive Director (1953-71) Trilateral Commission North American secretary and coordinator, fluent in Russian, toured the Soviet Union in the late 1950's to learn what the people thought of their Government, the United States and the possibility of war, his impressions were recalled in The New York Times Magazine in January 1958

John J. McCloy - CFR Director, Chairman (1953-72) was a lawyer and banker, Assistant Secretary of War during World War II, president of the World Bank, and

U.S. High Commissioner for Germany, United States presidential advisor, served on the Warren Commission, and was a member of the foreign policy establishment group of elders called "The Wise Men."

Arthur H. Dean - CFR Director (1955-72) New York lawyer and diplomat, served as a key advisor to numerous U.S. presidents, Chairman and Senior Partner of Sullivan & Cromwell, where he worked closely with John Foster Dulles, chief U.S. negotiator at Panmunjeom where he helped negotiate the treaty that ended the Korean War, and also helped draft and negotiate the Nuclear Test Ban Treaty in 1963, the Asia Society, delegate to the United Nations

Charles M. Spofford - CFR Director (1955-72) U.S. deputy on the North Atlantic Treaty council

Adlai E. Stevenson - CFR Director (1958-62) Illinois Governor, UN Ambassador to United States

William C. Foster - CFR Director (1959-72) director of the U.S. Arms Control and Disarmament Agency

Caryl P. Haskins - CFR Director (1961-75) President, Research Director, and Chairman of the Board of Haskins Laboratories, Director, E.I. du Pont de Nemours, Research Professor, Union College, 1937-1955. In 1956, President of the Carnegie Institution of Washington

James A. Perkins - CFR Director (1963-79) president of Cornell University

William P. Bundy - CFR Director (1964-84) member of the CIA and foreign affairs, analyst for the Central Intelligence Agency, chief of staff for the Office of National Estimates, director for Eisenhower's Commission on National Goals, deputy to Assistant Secretary for International Security Affairs Paul Nitze and worked for the Secretary of the Navy, Assistant Secretary of State for East Asian and Pacific affairs, Honorary American Secretary General of the Bilderberg Meetings from 1975 to 1980

Carroll L. Wilson - CFR Director, Vice Chairman (1964-79) Professor MIT

Gabriel Hauge - CFR Director, Treasurer (1964-81) economics instructor at Harvard University, worked at the Federal Reserve Bank of New York, professor of economics at Princeton University, active member of the United States Navy Reserve, economist with the State Banking Department in New York State, assistant Editor of Business Week magazine, Economic Advisor to the 1948 Presidential campaign of Thomas Dewey, Dwight D. Eisenhower's campaign staff as a research director for Citizens for Eisenhower, assistant to the President for Economic Affairs, chairman of the Board of Directors of Manufacturers Hanover Trust Company

Douglas Dillon - CFR Director (1965-78) US National Security Council, US Ambassador to France, US Secretary of State

Henry R. Labouisse - CFR Director (1965-74) State Department and United Nations official, headed Unicef, the United Nations Children's Fund, Ambassador to Greece

Lucian W. Pye - CFR Director (1966-82) advised the Department of State and the National Security Council in China-related matters, served as an advisor to Democratic presidential candidates, Senators John F. Kennedy and Henry M. Jackson, and urged both men to pursue a muscular foreign policy, an early proponent of the Vietnam War, leader and eventually acting chairman with the National Committee on United States-China Relations

Robert V. Roosa - CFR Director (1966-81) Under Secretary of the Treasury for monetary affairs, general partner of Brown Brothers Harriman & Company

Bill Moyers - CFR Director (1967-74) US Press Secretary, Journalist cbs, nbc, msnbc, pbs

Alfred C. Neal - CFR Director (1967-76) economist whose interest in developing the global economy influenced United States trade policy

Cyrus R. Vance - CFR Director, Vice Chairman (1968-87) US Deputy Secretary of defense, US Secretary of the Army, US Secretary of State

Hedley Donovan - CFR Director (1969-79) editor in chief of Time Inc. responsible for all publications of Time Inc., including Time, Life, Fortune, Sports Illustrated, Money, and People, became a senior adviser to President Jimmy Carter, worked as a reporter at The Washington Post for five years and then worked as a naval officer in World War II, published his first book Roosevelt to Reagan: A Reporter's Encounters with Nine Presidents in 1985 under the publication company Harper & Row

Najeeb E. Halaby - CFR Director (1970-72) U.S. State Department's civil aviation advisor to King Ibn Saud of Saudi Arabia, aide to Secretary of Defense James, joined Laurance Rockefeller's family office in 1953 reviewing investments in civil aviation, Administrator of the Federal Aviation Administration, proponent for the creation of the U.S. Department of Transportation, which occurred during his time in the Lyndon Johnson administration, CEO, and chairman Pan Am

Bayless Manning - CFR Director, President (1971-77) Yale Editor-in-chief of the Law Journal

Marshall D. Shulman - CFR Director (1972-77) information officer for the U.S. mission to the U.N., special advisor on Soviet affairs to Secretary of State Cyrus R. Vance, associate director of the Russian Research Center at Harvard University

Elizabeth Drew - CFR Director (1972-77) Washington correspondent for The Atlantic Monthly, and The New Yorker, made regular appearances on "Agronsky and Company," and hosted her own interview program for PBS, was a panelist for the first debate in the 1976 U.S. Presidential election, and moderated the debate between the Democratic candidates for the nomination in the 1984 race

Zbigniew Brzezinski - CFR Director (1972-77) United States National Security Advisor

Paul C. Warnke - CFR Director (1972-77) assistant secretary of defense for international affairs, founded the law firm Clifford, Warnke, Glass, McIlwain & Finney, chief U.S. negotiator to the Strategic Arms

Limitation Talks (SALT) with the Soviet Union, head of the Arms Control and Disarmament Agency (ACDA) , led the U.S. delegation to the SALT II negotiations

Martha Redfield Wallace - CFR Director (1972-82) director of Bristol, director of the Chemical Bank, board of American Express, surveillance committee of the New York Stock Exchange. Director of the exchange from 1977 until 1983, Rhodes Scholar Panel

W. Michael Blumenthal - CFR Director (1972-84) served as United States Secretary of the Treasury under President Jimmy Carter from 1977-1979

Peter G. Peterson - CFR Director, Treasurer, Chairman (1973-2007) United States Secretary of Commerce, Chairman and CEO of Bell & Howell, Chairman and CEO of Lehman Brothers, co-founded the private equity firm, the Blackstone Group, succeeded David Rockefeller as Chairman of the Council on Foreign Relations in 1985 and served until his retirement in 2007

Elliot L. Richardson - CFR Director (1974-75) Massachusetts Attorney General, LT Gov. Mass., US Ambassador to the United Kingdom, US undersecretary of war, US Secretary of Health, Education and welfare, US Secretary of Defense, US Attorney General, US Secretary of Commerce

Robert O. Anderson - CFR Director (1974-80) founded Atlantic Richfield Oil Co.

Edward K. Hamilton - CFR Director, President (1974-83) co-founder HR&A Hamilton, Rabinovitz & Associates, Inc., First Deputy Mayor of New York, Senior Member of the National Security Council staff in the White House

Nicholas deB. Katzenbach - CFR Director (1975-86) U.S. Department of Justice as Assistant Attorney General of the Office of Legal Counsel, Deputy Attorney General, Attorney General of the United States, Under Secretary of State, attorney-advisor in the Office of General Counsel to the Secretary of the Air Force.

Franklin Hall Williams - CFR Director (1975-83) lawyer, government administrator, and ambassador, CIVIL RIGHTS MOVEMENT, As an attorney with the National Association for the Advancement of Colored People (NAACP)

Paul A. Volcker - CFR Director (1975-88) full-time economist Federal Reserve Bank of New York, financial economist with the Chase Manhattan Bank, U.S. Treasury Department as director of financial analysis, deputy under-secretary for monetary affairs, Vice President of Chase Manhattan Bank, under-secretary of the Treasury for international monetary affairs, played an important role in the decisions leading to the U.S. suspension of gold convertibility in 1971, which resulted in the collapse of the Bretton Woods system. President of the Federal Reserve Bank of New York, chairman of the Federal Reserve

Theodore M. Hesburgh - CFR Director (1976-85) served as Notre Dame's President for 35 years (1952–87)

Lane Kirkland - CFR Director (1976-86) president of the American Federation of Labor – Congress of Industrial Organizations (AFL-CIO)

Lloyd N. Cutler - CFR Director (1977-79) founder Wilmer, Cutler & Pickering, directs 500 lawyers representing or lobbying for the world's most powerful corporations and industrial groups. The firm's clients included the Automobile Manufacturers Association and the Pharmaceutical Research and Manufacturers of America, and companies that included I.B.M., ABC, CBS, NBC, Cigna, many airlines, major newspapers, banks and professional sports teams. President Carter's counsel in 1979, working on issues arising from the Iranian hostage crisis, the SALT II treaty negotiations and the Soviet invasion of Afghanistan

Winston Lord - CFR Director, President (1977-85) key figure in the restoration of relations between the United States and China in 1972, United States National Security Council's planning staff, special assistant to National Security Advisor Henry Kissinger, U.S. delegation during President Richard Nixon's historic visit to China, State Department's Director of Policy Planning and top policy adviser on China, United States Ambassador to China, Assistant Secretary of State for East Asian and Pacific Affairs

George H. W. Bush - CFR Director (1977-79) the 41st President of the United States

Henry A. Kissinger - CFR Director (1977-79) National Security Advisor and Secretary of State in the administrations of Presidents Richard Nixon and Gerald Ford, regular participant in meetings of the annual invitation-only Bilderberg Group

Marina V.N. Whitman - CFR Director (1977-87) served on Richard Nixon's Council of Economic Advisers

Philip L. Geyelin - CFR Director (1977-87) veteran foreign correspondent for the The Wall Street Journal, Washington Post deputy editorial page editor

Stephen Stamas - CFR Director (1977-89) US Budget Bureau as a loan officer in the Development Loan Fund, Deputy Assistant Secretary for Financial Policy in the US Department of Commerce, Exxon Corporation in a number of financial, supply, corporate planning and public affairs positions

C. Peter McColough - CFR Director, Treasurer (1978-87) joint creater and owner of the Xerox Corporation, former Chief Executive Officer and Chairman of the Board at Xerox, treasurer of the Democratic National Committee, Chairman of United Way of America, and served on the Board of Trustees at New York Stock Exchange, Bank of New York, Wachovia, Citibank, and Union Carbide Corporation.

Graham T. Allison, Jr. - CFR Director (1979-88) American political scientist and professor at Harvard, had some influence on the foreign policy of the administration of President Jimmy Carter, a leading analyst of U.S. national security and defense policy, with a special interest in nuclear weapons and terrorism

Richard L. Gelb - CFR Director (1979-88) director of the New York Life Insurance Company, The New York Times, Bessemer Securities Corporation and Federal Reserve Bank of New York, Director of Bristol-Myers Squibb Company

William D. Ruckelshaus - CFR Director (1979-83) first head of the Environmental Protection Agency (EPA), acting Director of the Federal Bureau of Investigation, Deputy Attorney General of the United States, EPA Administrator. In 1985, joined Perkins Coie, World Commission on Environment and Development set up by the United Nations, Chairman and Chief Executive Officer of Browning Ferris Industries of Houston, Texas. U.S. envoy in the implementation of the Pacific Salmon Treaty; Chairman of the Salmon Recovery Funding Board for the State of Washington, United States Commission on Ocean Policy

George P. Shultz - CFR Director (1980-82) American economist, statesman, and businessman, served as the United States Secretary of Labor, U.S. Secretary of the Treasury, U.S. Secretary of State, professor of economics at MIT and the University of Chicago, serving as Dean of the University of Chicago Graduate School of Business, an president of Bechtel

James F. Hoge, Jr. - CFR Director, Editor of Foreign Affairs (1980-84) Washington correspondent for the Chicago Sun-Times, editor in chief and publisher. In 1984, president and publisher of the New York Daily

News, The Sun-Times won six Pulitzer Prizes during his tenure there, and the Daily News won one during his presidency

William D. Rogers - CFR Director (1980-90) U.S. Assistant Secretary of State for Inter-American Affairs, Undersecretary of State for Economic Affairs, under then-Secretary of State Henry Kissinger, founding members in 1982, and from 2004 until his death was vice chairman, of Kissinger's consulting firm Kissinger Associates, joined the law firm of Arnold, Fortas, & Porter (now Arnold & Porter)

Lewis T. Preston - CFR Director, Treasurer (1981-88) President of the World Bank from September 1991 until his death in May 1995

Walter B. Wriston - CFR Director (1981-87) chairman and CEO of Citicorp, chairman of President Ronald Reagan's Economic Policy Advisory Board, awarded the Presidential Medal of Freedom

Alan Greenspan - CFR Director (1982-88) Chairman of the Federal Reserve 1987-2008

Robert A. Scalapino - CFR Director (1982-89) founders and first chairman of the National Committee on United States – China Relations, served in U.S. Naval

Warren Christopher - CFR Director, Vice Chairman (1982-91) Secretary of State, Deputy Attorney General, Deputy Secretary of State, Senior Partner at O'Melveny & Myers in the firm's Century City, CA office.

Brent Scowcroft - CFR Director (1983-89) National Security Advisor

Alton Frye - CFR Director, Vice President, SR. Vice President, President (1983-89) Former State Department director of policy planning and lead U.S. official on Afghanistan and Northern Ireland, principal Middle East adviser to President George H.W. Bush

Clifton R. Wharton, Jr - CFR Director (1983-92) US Deputy Secretary of State

Harold Brown - CFR Director (1983-92) American scientist, U.S. Secretary of Defense, Director of Defense Research and Engineering, Secretary of the Air Force, took part in the strategic arms negotiations with the Soviet Union and supported (unsuccessfully), ratification of the SALT II treaty

Juanita M. Kreps - CFR Director (1983-92) US. Secretary of Commerce

Donald F. McHenry - CFR Director (1984-93) US Ambassador to the UN

William G. Hyland - CFR Director (1984-93) CIA's Berlin desk officer, briefed the agency's legendary director Allen Dulles, moved on to the CIA's Soviet desk, former deputy national security adviser, accompanied United States Secretary of State Henry Kissinger and President Richard Nixon to a summit in Moscow, Director of the Bureau of Intelligence, President's Foreign Intelligence Advisory Board

Jeane J. Kirkpatrick - CFR Director, Vice Chairman (1985-94) American ambassador, Ronald Reagan's foreign policy adviser, U.S. ambassador to the United Nations served on Reagan's Cabinet on the National Security Council, Foreign Intelligence Advisory Board, Defense Policy Review Board, and chaired the Secretary of Defense Commission on Fail Safe and Risk reduction of the Nuclear Command and Control System

B. R. Inman - CFR Director, Vice Chairman (1985-93) Chairman of the Federal Reserve Bank of Dallas, Director of Naval Intelligence, Defense Intelligence Agency served as Vice Director, Director of the National Security Agency, Deputy Director of the Central Intelligence Agency, Chairman and Chief Executive Officer of the Microelectronics and Computer Technology Corporation (MCC), Chairman, President and Chief Executive Officer of Westmark Systems, Inc.

Charles McC. Mathias, Jr. - CFR Director (1986-92) US House of Representatives MD. US Senator MD 1969-1987

Ruben F. Mettler - CFR Director (1986-92) served on the boards of Bank of America, Merck, Goodyear, Bechtel and Sola International, chief executive of TRW, a leader in the development of America's ballistic missile program

Peter Tarnoff - CFR Director, President (1986-92) Undersecretary of State for Political Affairs, Executive Secretary of the Department of State and Special Assistant to Secretaries of State Edmund Muskie and

Cyrus Vance, Director, Office of Research and Analysis for Western Europe, Special Assistant to Ambassador-at-Large Henry Cabot Lodge, Jr., Nigerian Analyst in the Bureau of Intelligence and Research, Deputy Chief of Mission at the American Embassy in Luxembourg, Principal Officer at the American Consulate General in Lyon, France, Special Assistant to the U.S. Ambassador to the Federal Republic of Germany, Special Assistant to the Chief of the American Delegation to the Paris Talks on Vietnam, Special Assistant to the Deputy U.S. Ambassador, U.S. Ambassador Saigon, Vietnam, Political Officer at the U.S. Embassy in Lagos, Nigeria

William H. Gleysteen, Jr. - CFR Director (1987-89) United States ambassador to South Korea.

Richard B. Cheney - CFR Director (1987-95) White House Chief of Staff, U.S. House of Representatives from Wyoming, House Minority Whip, Secretary of Defense, oversaw the 1991 Operation Desert Storm, Cheney was chairman and CEO of Halliburton Company, 46th Vice President of the United States

Glenn E. Watts - CFR Director (1987-90) trustee for the Ford Foundation, member of the Tri-Lateral Commission, member of the Aspen Institute, led the Communications Workers of America

Karen Elliott House - CFR Director (1987) journalist and former executive at the Wall Street Journal and its parent company Dow Jones, served as President of Dow Jones International and then publisher of the WSJ

James E. Burke - CFR Director, Treasurer (1987-90) the chief executive officer (CEO) of Johnson & Johnson

Robert F. Erburu - CFR Director (1987) Director and Chairman, The Times Mirror Co, Director the U.S. Chamber of Commerce, Director the Ahmanson Foundation, Director the Getty Trust

Margaret Osmer-McQuade - CFR Director, Vice President (1987-93) President of Qualitas International, Director of Washington Mutual Inc., Director of Riverside Capital International LLC. Trustee Emeritus of Cornell University, Director of Dime Bancorp Inc. and Anchor Bancorp and/or the Board of Directors of Anchor Savings Bank FSB & Dime Savings

James D. Robinson III - CFR Director (1988-91) chief executive officer of American Express Co., general partner and co-founder of RRE Ventures, president of J.D. Robinson, Inc., chairman of Violy, Byorum & Partners, serves on the Boards of Directors of The Coca-Cola Company Inc. honorary trustee of the Brookings Institution, served as co-chairman of the Business Roundtable and chairman of the Advisory Committee on Trade Policy and Negotiations

Strobe Talbott - CFR Director (1988-93) Deputy Secretary of State , American foreign policy analyst associated with Yale University and the Brookings Institution, journalist associated with Time magazine

Thomas S. Foley - CFR Director (1988-94) United States House of Representatives representing Washington's 5th congressional district, 57th Speaker of the United States House of Representatives, United States Ambassador to Japan

Alice M. Rivlin - CFR Director (1989-92) Vice Chairman of the Federal Reserve, Director of the congressional Budget Office

Joshua Lederberg - CFR Director (1989) American molecular biologist known for his work in genetics, artificial intelligence, and space exploration, 1958 Nobel Prize in Physiology or Medicine

William S. Cohen - CFR Director (1989) Secretary of Defense, Senate Armed Services Committee and the Governmental Affairs Committee, Senate Intelligence Committee

John S. Reed - CFR Director (1989-92) Chairman of the New York Stock Exchange, served as Chairman and CEO of Citicorp, Citibank, and post-merger, Citigroup

John L. Clendenin - CFR Director (1989-94) Chairman of the Board of Directors of Powerwave, Chairman Emeritus of BellSouth Corporation, President of Southern Bell

Thomas R. Donahue - CFR Director (1990) Secretary-Treasurer of the AFL-CIO

William J. Crowe, Jr. - CFR Director (1990-93) United States Navy Admiral, Chairman of the Joint Chiefs of Staff, ambassador to the United Kingdom

Richard C. Holbrooke - CFR Director (1991-96) Assistant Secretary of State, Special Representative for Afghanistan and Pakistan, U.S. Ambassador to Germany, brokered a peace agreement among the warring factions in Bosnia that led to the signing of the Dayton Peace Accords, U.S. Ambassador to the United Nations

Robert D. Hormats - CFR Director (1991) Under Secretary of State for Economic, Business, and Agricultural Affairs, Vice Chairman of Goldman Sachs (International), Senior Deputy Assistant Secretary, Assistant Secretary of State at the Bureau of Economic and Business Affairs, Ambassador and Deputy U.S. Trade Representative, senior staff member for International Economic Affairs on the United States National Security Council senior economic adviser to Henry Kissinger, General Brent Scowcroft and Zbigniew Brzezinski, manage the Nixon administration's opening of diplomatic relations with China's communist government

Donna E. Shalala - CFR Director (1992-93) US Secretary of health and human services, President University of Miami

Karen N. Horn - CFR Director (1992-95) Lead Director for Eli Lilly Inc., managing director of Marsh, Inc., senior managing director and head of international private banking at Bankers Trust Company; chairman and chief executive officer of Bank One, Cleveland, N.A.; president of the Federal Reserve Bank of Cleveland; treasurer of Bell Telephone Company of Pennsylvania; and vice president of First National Bank of Boston, director of

T. Rowe Price Mutual Funds; Simon Property Group, Inc.; and Norfolk Southern Corporation and vice chairman of the U.S.-Russia Investment Foundation, served on the board of Fannie Mae and Georgia-Pacific Corporation

James R. Houghton - CFR Director (1992-96) Chairman of the Board of Corning

Maurice R. Greenberg - CFR Director, Vice Chairman (1992-94) chairman and CEO of American International Group (AIG), social friend and client of Henry Kissinger, appointed Kissinger as chairman of AIG's International Advisory Board, Trustee Emeritus of the Rockefeller University, and is an honorary Trustee of the Museum of Modern Art, all three institutions founded by the Rockefeller family, Chairman, Deputy Chairman and Director of the Federal Reserve Bank of New York, Vice-Chairman of the Board of Directors of the National Committee on United States – China Relations

Charlayne Hunter-Gault - CFR Director (1992) The New York Times as a metropolitan reporter specializing in coverage of the urban African American community, joined The MacNeil/Lehrer Report in 1978 as a correspondent, and became The News Hour's national correspondent, worked in Johannesburg, South Africa as National Public Radio's (NPR) chief correspondent in Africa

Kenneth W. Dam - CFR Director (1992) Deputy Secretary of the Treasury, senior fellow of the Brookings Institution, Assistant Director for national security and international affairs at the Office of

Management and Budget, Executive Director of the White House Council on Economic Policy, Deputy Secretary of State, vice president for law and external relations at IBM, served as president and CEO of the United Way, member of the board of Alcoa

John E. Bryson - CFR Director (1992) Chief Executive Officer, and President of Edison International, director of The Boeing Company, W. M. Keck Foundation, and The Walt Disney Company, a Director/Trustee for three funds in the Western Asset funds complex, a trustee of California Institute of Technology, and co-Chair of the Pacific Council on International Policy

Paul A. Allaire - CFR Director (1992) CEO and Chairman of Xerox Corporation, chairman of GlaxoSmithKline's remuneration committee

E. Gerald Corrigan - CFR Director (1993-95) President of the Federal Reserve Bank of New York and Vice-Chairman of the Federal Open Market Committee, partner and managing director in the Office of the Chairman at Goldman Sachs, chairman of GS Bank USA, the bank holding company of Goldman Sachs, member of the Group of Thirty

Richard N. Cooper - CFR Director (1993-94) senior staff economist on the Council of Economic Advisers, Deputy Assistant Secretary of State for International Monetary Affairs in the United States Department of State, Under-Secretary of State for Economic Affairs, chairman of the Federal Reserve Bank of Boston, chairman of the National Intelligence Council

Garrick Utley - CFR Director (1993) weekend anchor on NBC Nightly News, hosted newsmagazine-style programs for NBC News, In the UK he covered the February 1974 British General Election, and appeared on the BBC election night program, moderated NBC's long-running public affairs discussion program Meet the Press, while simultaneously hosting the newly-debuted Sunday version of the Today Show

Leslie H. Gelb - CFR Director, President (1993) correspondent for The New York Times

Robert E. Allen - CFR Director, President (1993) CEO, Chairman and president of AT&T, board of Pepsico

Frank G. Zarb - CFR Director (1994-96) the chairman of the NASDAQ stock exchange

Helene L. Kaplan - CFR Director (1994-96) director of Exxon Mobil, MetLife, Inc. and Metropolitan Life Insurance, May Department Stores Corporation, JPMorgan Chase and Company and its predecessor companies, Verizon Communications, Inc., member of the Carnegie Commission on Science, Technology, and Government and chaired its Task Force on Judicial and Regulatory Decision Making, member of the U.S. Secretary of State's Advisory Committee on South Africa, member of New York Governor Cuomo's Task Force on Life and the Law

Carla A. Hills - CFR Director (1994) US Secretary of housing and urban development, US Trade Representative, primary U.S. negotiator of the North American Free Trade Agreement (NAFTA)

Robert B. Zoellick - CFR Director (1994) eleventh president of the World Bank, managing director of Goldman Sachs, United States Deputy Secretary of State, U.S. Trade Representative

Frank Savage - CFR Director (1995) Enron Board of Directors

Jessica P. Einhorn - CFR Director (1995) U.S. Deputy Secretary of Defense, member of the Board of Directors of Time Warner, Inc., managing director at the World Bank

George Soros - CFR Director (1995) Chairman of the Soros Fund Management and the Open Society Institute

William J. McDonough - CFR Director (1995) vice chairman and special advisor to the chairman at Merrill Lynch & Co. Inc., president and chief executive officer of the Federal Reserve Bank of New York, vice chairman and a permanent member of the Federal Open Market Committee (FOMC), board of directors of the Bank for International Settlements and as chairman of the Basel Committee on Banking Supervision. Board member First Chicago Corporation and its bank, First National Bank of Chicago, U.S. Navy, U.S. State Department, chairman of the Investment Committee for the United Nations Joint Staff Pension Fund, co-chairman of the United Nations Association of the United States of America (UNA-USA), member of the Group of Thirty

George J. Mitchell - CFR Director (1995) U.S. Special Envoy for Middle East Peace under the Obama administration, United States Senator who served as the

Senate Majority Leader, chairman of The Walt Disney Company, chairman of the international law firm DLA Piper, Chancellor of Queen's University in Belfast, Northern Ireland and was the main investigator in both Mitchell Reports

David J. Vidal - CFR Director (1995) Continental Insurance, the New York City Partnership, the U.S. Department of State, the New York Times, and The Associated Press

Hannah Holborn Gray - CFR Director (1995) Director, Board Member or Trustee of various institutions, including the Harvard Corporation, the Yale Corporation, the Smithsonian Institution, JP Morgan Chase, the Andrew W. Mellon Foundation , United States Ambassador to the Court of St. James

Les Aspin - CFR Director (1995) United States Representative, United States Secretary of Defense

Louis V. Gerstner, Jr. - CFR Director (1995) chief executive officer of IBM, CEO of RJR Nabisco, American Express.

Mario L. Baeza - CFR Director (1995) founder and controlling shareholder of the Baeza Group LLC, chairman of V-me Media Inc., founder and chairman of AJM Records, Board of Directors of Air Products and Chemicals, Inc., lead director of Tommy Hilfiger Corporation, Board of Directors of the Ariel Mutual Funds Complex, Board of the Israel Discount Bank of New York, Board of Brown Shoe Company, Inc.

Michael P. Peters - CFR Director (1995) Chief of Staff, United States Military, Battalion Commander in Operations Just Cause and Desert Shield, Special Assistant to the Chairman of the Joint Chiefs of Staff, attaché in Moscow, Executive Officer/Platoon Leader, Vietnam

Lee Cullum - CFR Director (1996) award-winning columnist who contributes regularly to the Dallas Morning News, She has done frequent commentary on the News Hour with Jim Lehrer, she is also on National Public Radio, editor of the editorial page of the Dallas Times Herald, and editor of a Dallas magazine

Henry M. Paulson, Jr. – CFR Member (Current) 74th United States Treasury Secretary, Chairman and Chief Executive Officer of Goldman Sachs

Diane Sawyer - CFR Member (Current) anchor of ABC World News. Previously, co-anchor of ABC News's morning news program, Good Morning America

Peter Bakstansky - CFR Member (Current) senior vice president of the Federal Reserve Bank of New York and a member of the bank's management committee after 30 years

Reginald Bartholomew - CFR Member (Current) United States Ambassador to Lebanon, Spain and Italy, member of the United States National Security

David O Rielly - CFR Member (Current) former chairman and CEO of Chevron Corporation

Stansfield M. Turner - CFR Member (Current) Admiral and Director of Central Intelligence

Vaughan Turekian - CFR Member (Current) Chief International Officer American Association for the Advancement of Science, served as Special Assistant to the Under Secretary of State for Global Affairs

Ko-Yung Tung - CFR Member (Current) Vice President and General Counsel of the World Bank and as Secretary General of ICSID, senior partner of O'Melveny & Myers and head of its Global Practice Group, published chapter entitled "Foreign Investors vs Sovereign States: Towards a Global Framework, BIT by BIT" in International Economic Law and National Autonomy (Cambridge University Press, 2010)

Condoleezza Rice - CFR Member (Current) 66th United States Secretary of State, President Bush's National Security Advisor

John D. Negroponte - CFR Member (Current) research fellow and lecturer in international affairs at Yale University's Jackson Institute for Global Affairs, United States Deputy Secretary of State and as the first ever Director of National Intelligence, United States ambassador in Honduras, Mexico, and the Philippines, U.S. permanent representative to the United Nations, ambassador to Iraq

Steven C. Rockefeller - CFR Member, son of former United States Vice President Nelson Aldrich Rockefeller, dean of Middlebury College, trustee of the Asian Cultural Council and an advisory trustee of the

Rockefeller Brothers Fund, director of the Rockefeller Philanthropy Advisors

Nicholas Rockefeller - CFR Member (Current) vice chairman and chief legal officer of the RockVest Group of Investors, involved in various banking and commercial projects in China and worldwide, member the International Institute of Strategic Studies, the Advisory Board of RAND, the Corporate Advisory Board of the Pacific Council on International Relations, the Board of the Western Justice Center Foundation, and the Central China Development Council, served as a participant in the World Economic Forum and the Aspen Institute, serves as a director of the Pacific Rim Cultural Foundation, practice includes transactions with China's largest banks, energy companies, communications entities and real estate enterprises as well as with China's principal cities and leading provinces, chosen as a board member of the Central China Construction and Development Commission and as a director of the Xiwai International School of Shanghai International University

David Rockefeller Jr. - CFR Member (Current) son of David Rockefeller, Rockefeller Foundation board of trustees

Chapter 8

"Joined at the hip - US Intelligence and the CFR"

In an article depicting the history of the CFR posted on their website this excerpt sheds some light on the nature of the association that has developed between the CFR and US intelligence.

"MORE THAN TWO YEARS before the Japanese attack on Pearl Harbor, the research staff of the Council on Foreign Relations had started to envision a venture that would dominate the life of the institution for the demanding years ahead. With the memory of the Inquiry in focus, they conceived a role for the Council in the formulation of national policy. On September 12, 1939, as Nazi Germany invaded Poland, Armstrong and Mallory entrained to Washington to meet with Assistant Secretary of State George S. Messersmith. At that time the Department of State could command few resources for study, research, policy planning, and initiative; on such matters, the career diplomats on the eve of World War II were scarcely better off than had been their predecessors when America entered World War I. The men from the Council proposed a discreet venture reminiscent of the Inquiry: a program of independent analysis and study that would guide American foreign policy in the coming years of war and the challenging new world that would emerge after. The project became known as the War and Peace Studies. "The matter is strictly confidential," wrote

Bowman, *"because the whole plan would be 'ditched' if it became generally known that the State Department is working in collaboration with any outside group...* Such were the effects of the upheavals of war upon the habits of society. The primary function of the Council on Foreign Relations during World War II proceeded in **rigid secrecy**, remote from the slightest awareness of most of the Council's 663 members, who were not themselves personally involved."

In their own words this is the story of how the CFR became deeply rooted in the US Intelligence community. On September 12, 1939 Hamilton Fish Armstrong, Editor of Foreign Affairs, and Walter H. Mallory, Executive Director of the CFR, paid a visit to the State Department. The Council proposed forming groups of experts to proceed with research in the general areas of security, armament, economic, political, and territorial problems. The project (1939-1945) was called "Council on Foreign Relations War and Peace Studies" Hamilton Fish Armstrong was Executive Director. Funded by the Rockefeller foundation these investigations by members of the CFR were broken into four categories economic and financial, security and armaments, territorial, and political. They were marked classified and top secret given to the State Department and circulated among the proper parties. Basically what was taking place was this private group was advancing their agenda using their interpretation of foreign affairs to influence foreign policies of the government. The CFR members that worked on the War and Peace Studies were mobilized into government service once the US became involved with the war.

One of the most influential of these was Sullivan and Cromwell Attorney Allen Dulles who had been a Director of the CFR since 1927. During the War he was working out of a base in Switzerland as part of the Office of Strategic Services (OSS) precursor to the CIA where he was able to actualize the ideology of the War and Peace Studies. Because of his affiliation with the CFR in 1953 Allen Dulles became the first civilian Director of the Central Intelligence Agency. The three previous Directors had military backgrounds. While at the helm of the CIA Dulles (1953-1961 *the longest term ever to be held by a director*) was instrumental in the overthrow of the Iranian government, the Guatemalan government, the formation of operation 40, the MK-Ultra mind control research project, operation Mockingbird, institution of the U-2 Spy plane and the attempted overthrow of Fidel Castro in Cuba. During his tenure America saw the creation of the Soviet Intelligent organization the KGB. A case by case study of these events shows not only a pattern of CFR inclusion but also its utter failure as an institute of foreign policy wisdom. There are basically only two conclusions to draw from these cases;

- The total incompetence of the CFR and other think tanks of foreign policy to represent the freedom of the constitutional American Republic, its citizens and the benevolent fair treatment of the people of the world.

OR

- The goals of these private organizations are not freedom and justice but the global accumulation of power above all national sovereignty.

The **1953 Iranian coup d'état (CIA OPERATION TPAJAX)**

William Knox D'Arcy an oil entrepreneur of the nineteenth century solicited the Persian Mozaffar ad-Din Shah Qajar, the fifth Qajarid Shah of Persia for his countries oil concessions. Because of the country's economic condition at the time the Shah signed what became known as the D'Arcy Oil Concession. In 1900 D'Arcy consented to finance a search for oil and minerals in Iran. D'Arcy would have the oil rights to the entire country except for five provinces in Northern Iran and the Iranian government was given a 16% stake of the oil company's annual profits. After seven years of toil D'Arcy finally struck oil on May 26 1908. In April 1909 D'Arcy became known as the director of the Anglo-Iranian Oil Company known today as British Petroleum or BP. By 1914 the British government had taken an interest in the Anglo-Iranian Oil Company because Britain was converting all of their ships from coal to oil. In an agreement with the company Britain paid 2.2 million pounds for a 51% stake in the company. By 1950 the Anglo-Iranian Oil Company was producing the majority of Europe's Oil.

In 1950 The American Oil interests had similar national agreements with Saudi Arabia and Venezuela. In what became known as the "Golden Gimmick" Harry Truman enacted in November a foreign tax credit deal between King Ibn Saud of Saudi Arabia and the Arabian-American Oil Company (ARAMCO). ARAMCO was a conglomerate of Standard oil, Exxon, Mobil and Texaco. King Ibn Saud and Juan Pablo Pérez Alfonzo of Venezuela acted in unison to get a better deal from the American oil conglomerates for their countries. The 50/50 deal gave the American oil companies a tax break equivalent to 50% of their profits on oil sales, the other 50% was diverted to King Ibn Saud by the US Treasury. This was done to keep these countries from nationalizing their oil supplies. Seeing this take place with the Americans the Iranian government began demanding from Britain a larger portion of the profits of the Anglo-Iranian Oil Company and an increased part in the administration of the company. British government officials rejected all demands by Iran to alter the current agreement. The arrangement was at the time Britain's most profitable asset and negotiations between the two countries collapsed.

In a bold move from the Majlis, the Iranian democratically elected parliament, the oil industry was nationalized by a unanimous vote. The measure was later approved by the Senate as well. On April 27, 1951 later that same month the Majlis appointed Mohammed Mossadeq, Prime Minister of Iran. Because of his popularity Mohammad Reza Shah Pahlavi was forced to accept his position.

The British government challenged the actions of Iran in the International Court of Justice but the case was declined. The Truman administration wanted to remain neutral, believing that Mossadeq's disdain for communism would cause Iran to remain an ally in the struggle against communism. Mossadeq was convinced that the revenues from the oil would bring prosperity to Iran and keep the communist influence of the Iranian Tudeh party from taking hold. Mossadeq's Democratic reform made him a hero to his people and was highly praised among the west as evidenced by his being chosen as Time man of the year over the other candidates Dean Acheson, Douglas MacArthur and

Dwight D. Eisenhower in 1951. In a speech on June 21,1951 Mossadeq stated:

"Our long years of negotiations with foreign countries... have yielded no results this far. With the oil revenues we could meet our entire budget and combat poverty, disease, and backwardness among our people. Another important consideration is that by the elimination of the power of the British company, we would also eliminate corruption and intrigue, by means of which the internal affairs of our country have been influenced. Once this tutelage has ceased, Iran will have achieved its economic and political independence. The Iranian state prefers to take over the production of petroleum itself. The company should do nothing else but return its property to the rightful owners. The nationalization law provide that 25% of the net profits on oil be set aside to meet all the legitimate claims of the company for compensation...It has been asserted abroad that Iran intends to expel the foreign oil experts from the country and then shut down oil installations. Not only is this allegation absurd; it is utter invention."

Mohammad Mossadeq

Mossadeq's aspirations for economic benefit from the nationalized oil company would not be achieved due the actions of the British Government and the world's oil cartel. In an effort to defeat Mossadeq, Britain imposed sanctions against Iran's oil production, increased their naval presence in the Persian Gulf and began to draw plans for a full scale military assault. The US strongly opposed Britain's plan for military intervention fearing involvement from the Soviets. The world's oil cartel (Standard oil, Exxon, Texaco,

Chevron etc.) was also concerned that Iran's nationalization of the oil industry would lead other nations to follow suit. They were concerned that a domino effect would bring about loss of control and profits for them so they sided with Britain. To further Iran's economic collapse Britain removed its entire company's oil technician staff from Iran. This left the country without enough qualified professionals to run the operation. Oil production in Iran dropped 95 percent from 241 million barrels in 1950 to 10 million barrels in 1952. Britain doubled their production in Saudi Arabia, Kuwait and Iraq, to make up for lost production in Iran so that no hardship was felt in Britain.

In late 1952 British Intelligence agents Christopher Montague Woodhouse, Samuel Falle, John Bruce Lockhart and CIA agents Kermit Roosevelt (son of Theodore Roosevelt and nephew of FDR), John H. Leavitt, Jown W. Pendleton and James A. Darling met in Washington to discuss a plan to overthrow Mohammad Mossedeq as Prime Minister and replace him with someone more sympathetic to the British Anglo-Iranian Oil Company. With the Election of Present Eisenhower policy towards Iran moved in favor of Britain. Eisenhower was convinced by his State Department lead by John Foster Dulles that the result of the oil boycott would be the collapse of the Iranian economy and the eventual control of the Soviets through the Tudeh party.

Dean Acheson admitted in response to President Eisenhower's claim. *"Throughout the crisis, the "communist danger" was more of a rhetorical device than a real issue—i.e. it was part of the cold-war discourse ...The Tudeh was no match for the armed tribes and the 129,000-man military. What is more, the*

British and Americans had enough inside information to be confident that the party had no plans to initiate armed insurrection. At the beginning of the crisis, when the Truman administration was under the impression a compromise was possible, Acheson had stressed the communist danger, and warned if Mosaddegh was not helped, the Tudeh would take over. The (British) Foreign Office had retorted that the Tudeh was no real threat. But, in August 1953, when the Foreign Office echoed the Eisenhower administration's claim that the Tudeh was about to take over, Acheson now retorted that there was no such communist danger. Acheson was honest enough to admit that the issue of the Tudeh was a smokescreen."

The 1953 Coup in Iran, *Science & Society*, Vol. 65, No. 2, Summer 2001, pp.182–215"

British Intelligence composed a plan to remove Mossadeq calling it Operation Boot. The plan was given to Kermit Roosevelt who took it to Allen Dulles. Dulles modified the plan and renamed it Operation TPAJAX it was composed of a four part plan.

1. A propaganda campaign to make Mohammad Mosseq appear to be a communist.
2. Encourage the opposition in Iran to create Disturbances.
3. Pressure Mohammad Reza Shah Pahlavi to remove Mossadeq as Prime Minister and appoint a new Prime Minister.
4. Give support to General Fazlollah Zahedi as the new Prime Minister.

The plan was put into full force on August 1, 1953 with the arrival of Norman Schwarzkopf to meet with The Shah and Zahedi. Schwarzkopf assured them of total American support and produced a suitcase containing 5 million dollars in cash to finance the operation. Kermit Roosevelt met with the Shah later the same day to go over operation TPAJAX and it execution. The Shah issued an executive decree removing Mossadeq and appointing Zahedi to the post. On August 15 The commander of the Shah's Imperial Guard along with truckloads of soldiers stormed Mossedeq's home to serve him with the decree. Mossedeqs guards overpowered the Shah's Imperial Guard and Mossadeq sent his guards to find and arrest Zahedi who was hiding in the US Embassy while the Shah fled to Bagdad.

Taking advantage of the unrest Roosevelt hired a mob to pose as members of the communist tudeh party to riot and destroy property down the streets of Tehran. The CIA began bribing members of the military and police to refrain from the conflict. Two days later on August 19 the same mob armed with clubs and knives ascended on Mossadeq's house. Zahedi left the US Embassy to arrive at the state radio station to announce himself as the new Prime Minister. The Shah's Imperial Guard then joined the mob at Mossadeq's home but Mossadeq had escaped. He later surrendered to the Shah's forces. The conflict between the Imperial Guard, Mossedeq's guards and the mob had taken 300 lives. Martial law was called by Zahedi while he collected nationalist leaders and executed them. Mossadeq was spared execution at the request of the US but was sent to prison where he remained until his death in 1967.

For the US involvement in the coup against Iran Britain had to concede a 40 percent stake in the profits from the new agreement with the Shah. The agreement was to last for 25 years and had a 30 year extension. A good deal considering the US only paid 7 million to finance the CIA coup.

The Shah of Iran was finally removed from power and fled the state in 1979. He was perceived as an extravagant puppet of the United States. His government contributed to oppression, brutality and corruption. On 22 October 1979, at the request of David Rockefeller (President of the CFR), President Jimmy Carter reluctantly allowed the Shah into the United States to undergo surgical treatment. His prolonged stay in the U.S. was opposed by the Iranian government who demanded him to be extradited back to Iran for Trial. It is commonly reported this may have resulted in the Iran hostage crisis. When Iranians kidnapped U.S. officials from the embassy in Tehran, Americans were confused and resentful, not understanding how the Iranians could be so abominable against the U.S. officials. Americans felt the U.S. government had been supportive of the Shah of Iran. What the American people did not see was that the underlying animosity against the U.S. government was rooted in the horrible, anti-democratic act that was committed against Mohammad Mossadeq. Then the support of the Shah's oppressive government by the US produced in the Iranian people animosity towards what they saw as an American puppet regime. US foreign policy in Iran opposed democracy because it interfered with oil profits and used the fear propagated by the cold war to accomplish their ends. American leaders purposely supported a totalitarian government that oppressed the Iranian People for twenty five years.

U.S. Secretary of State Madeleine K. Albright stated:

"In 1953 the United States played a significant role in orchestrating the overthrow of Iran's popular Prime Minister, Mohammed Mossadegh. The Eisenhower Administration believed its actions were justified for strategic reasons; but the coup was clearly a setback for Iran's political development. And it is easy to see now why many Iranians continue to resent this intervention by America in their internal affairs."

Guatemala - Operation PB Success:

Through the collaboration of corrupt Latin American dictators the United Fruit Company (now the Dole Food Company) accumulated astonishing profits and capital. The United Fruit Company was built on the rich natural land resources of the Latin American Countryside and the cheap labor of the indigenous people of those countries. Those countries became known as the "Banana Republics". By the hand of corrupt leaders rural farmers were deprived of their property and became subjugated labor for the foreign owned banana and coffee companies. The small group of rich Latin American society businessmen and leaders worked with the American foreign companies to keep the labor force's wages low and keep them from gaining in the basic human rights category.

In 1944 Guatemalan educators and students began an attempt at gaining control of the country's dictatorship by a grass roots rebellion led by democratic ideology. The successful coup was characterized by sweeping social changes in politics and economics and the first ever elected President Juan Jose Arevalo. Arevalo's popularity with the common people helped him develop a democratic government like that of the United States. It promoted a new constitution that granted rights to the people such as freedom of speech and of the press and the right of women to vote. Arevalo instituted labor reforms like a forty hour work week, an establishment of a minimum wage and allowed labor unions to be created. This obviously caused a stir at the United Fruit Company's board meetings as their profits would be affected by the current reforms of the Guatemalan government. At this time the company was in possession of 42% of the land in Guatemala and held controlling interest in the seaport and electric utilities. This stake was given to the United Fruit Company in 1936 in an agreement between then Dictator Jorge Ubico and John Foster Dulles who was a board member of UFC and attorney for Sullivan and Cromwell and the older brother of Allen Dulles.

"Ubico showered United Fruit with concession agreements, including one in 1936 that his agents negotiated personally with John Foster Dulles. It gave the company a ninety-nine year lease on a vast tract of land along the rich pacific plain at Tiquisate, and guaranteed it an exemption from all taxes for the duration of the lease." Overthrow: America's Century of Regime Change from Hawaii to Iraq By Stephen Kinzer

In the 1951 election President Arévalo was succeeded by Jacobo Arbenz Guzmán with 65% of the popular vote. Like Arevalo, Arbenz also promoted reforms that antagonized the Guatemalan elite and foreign business especially the UFC. Arbenz enhanced the infrastructure by building an alternate port to the UFC controlled Puerto Barrios port. He planned to construct alternate electric utilities and highways that would compete with the railroad monopolies. Arbenz drove the final nail in his political coffin when he enacted Decree 900, a land reform act. He acknowledged that 2.2% of the country's population owned 70% of all agricultural land, but with only 12% of it being utilized. The agrarian act allowed the unused land to be redistributed among poor farmers that had their property taken by the methods of corrupt and racist past governments. Arbenz used the previous year's tax rolls to assess the value of the property for payment to the owners for the land. A Time magazine article describes the details of the land confiscation purchase by the Guatemalan government of the UFC tract of uncultivated land.

"The Communists and agrarian reformers who run Guatemala's government grabbed 233,973 acres of the United Fruit Co.'s best banana reserve lands at Tiquisate last year, and blandly offered the company $594,572 in 25-year government bonds as payment. The company, which values the land at $15,854,849, cried "confiscation," and asked the U.S. Government for help."
May 3 1954 Time Magazine

What the Time magazine article did not print was the way the land was acquired by UFC in the agreement arranged by Ubico and Dulles. Nor the fact that the land was exempt from taxes showing the land to be undervalued by the tax documents of previous years. Arbenz had based his offer on the estimated value the United Fruit Company itself used in its tax declarations. In April 1954 the U.S. State Department demanded the Árbenz government pay the United Fruit Company $15,854,849. Guatemala refused to pay the amount stating it was a violation of its sovereignty. On the board of the United Fruit Company were both Dulles brothers. In 1954 John Foster Dulles - U.S. Secretary of State and Allen Welsh Dulles - Director of the CIA and the United Fruit Company hired "the father of public relations" Edward Bernays and his propaganda firm to run a major public relations campaign to convince the American people and the U.S. government that Guatemala was a communist threat.

"It began with enviable connections to the Eisenhower administration. Secretary of State John Foster Dulles and his former New York law firm, Sullivan and Cromwell, had long represented the company. Allen Dulles, head of the CIA, had served on UFCO's board of trustees. Ed Whitman, the company's top public relations officer, was the husband of Ann Whitman, President Eisenhower's private secretary. (Ed Whitman produced a film, "Why the Kremlin Hates Bananas," that pictured UFCO fighting in the front trenches of the cold war.) The fruit firm's success in linking the taking of its lands to the evil of international communism was later described by one UFCO official as "the Disney version of the episode." But the company's efforts paid off. It picked up the expenses of journalists who traveled to Guatemala to learn United Fruit's side of the crisis, and some of the most respected North American publications - including the New York Times, New York Herald Tribune, and New Leader - ran stories that pleased the company. A UFCO public relations official later observed that his firm helped condition North American readers to accept the State Department's version of the Arbenz regime as Communist-controlled and the U.S.-planned invasion as wholly Guatemalan." (Quoted from Inevitable

Revolutions - The United States in Central America
by Walter La Feber, 2nd ed. 1993, pp. 120-121.

In an interview with CNN, CIA agent Howard
Hunt remarked that the United Fruit companies
lobbying campaign was a contributive factor in making
policy.

In declassified CIA documents we read how
CIA Headquarters created memos with titles like
"Guatemalan Communist Personnel to be disposed of
during Military Operations," marking those for
elimination "through Executive Action. A list of 58
names was erased from the declassified documents.
PBSUCCESS, authorized by President Eisenhower
allocated $2.7 million tax dollars for "psychological
warfare and political action" and "subversion."
Allen Dulles chose Carlos Armas who attended
academy with Árbenz to lead the coup. The CIA began
applying pressure on Arbenz and his government. They
created a base of operations in Florida to train rebels
and recruit operatives. A radio station was set up for
public relations. Arbenz began to suspect that a military
operation was being mounted against him and
attempted to buy military supplies first from Canada
and Germany but the sale was stopped by the CIA. He
was forced to make a deal to buy arms that had been
confiscated from Germany during World War II from
the Czech Republic, a Soviet Bloc country. When the
shipment reached Puerto Barrios, the CIA used it to
promote the idea that the Soviets were behind it all.
With America now convinced of the Soviet threat the
US Navy began patrols under the guise of protecting
Honduras from being invaded by Arbenz. On May 24
Operation HARDROCK BAKER by the U.S Navy
blockaded Guatemala's ports stopping all ships to

search for arms. Meanwhile propaganda leaflets were being dropped on Guatemala by air. The people of Guatemala now feared an impending military action against them.

The CIA sponsored radio station set up in Miami pretended to be broadcasting from the jungles of Guatemala with anti-government sentiment to lure those in Arbenz's military against him. On June 18 Castillo Armas's Army moved into Guatemala and was met with almost immediate failure and in a last stitch effort called for an air attack on the capital which also failed. Fearing that the total annihilation of the rebel forces would lead to an American attack Arbenz allowed Armas to escape into the jungle. Motivated by the fear of an American invasion an entire garrison of Arbenz military surrendered to Armas. Arbenz consigned himself to the fact that the military had buckled under the US threat and resigned as President fleeing the country.

In the successive CIA Operation PBHISTORY to search the Guatemalan archives for evidence of a Soviet controlled state found nothing despite searching through over 150,000 documents. This is a second case where foreign policy of the US was influenced by corporate interest and profits over the promotion of democracy. Deciding again to oppose the free democratic government created by the people of Guatemala and institute a totalitarian oppressive regime that would support US financial control.

Operation 40 (The struggle against Fidel Castro)

The absolute worst failure of American foreign policy towards any foreign nation would have to be Cuba prior to the rise of Fidel Castro. The pre-Castro days of Cuba were a time when the mafia ran the Cuban landscape. They created Las Vegas opulence with total control of the government. They paid Cuban dictator Fulgencio Batista millions of dollars to ensure that their operations were protected. An era that thrived on crime lords, U.S. money and corruption turned Cuba into the most fraudulent alliance of politics and decadence since ancient Rome. Crime bosses such as Lucky Luciano, Meyer Lansky and Sam Giancana were regular patrons of casino and night clubs that they controlled. The basic national infrastructure of Cuba was neglected, as well as education and welfare of the poor Cuban people whose income averaged $6.00 per week. Shortly after the Cuban Revolution John Fitzgerald Kennedy stated in a speech October 6, 1960:

"...The real question is: what should we have done? What did we do wrong? How did we permit the Communists to establish this foothold 90 miles away?

The answer is Four-Fold.

First, we refused to help Cuba meet its desperate need for economic progress. In 1953 the average Cuban family had an income of $6.00 a week. Fifteen to twenty per cent of the labor force was chronically unemployed.

Only a third of the homes in the island even had running water, and in the years which preceded the Castro revolution this abysmal standard of living was driven still lower as population expansion out-distanced economic growth.

Only 90 miles away stood the United States - their good neighbor - the richest nation on earth - its radios and newspapers and movies spreading the story of America's material wealth and surplus crops.

But instead of holding out a helping hand of friendship to the desperate people of Cuba, nearly all our aid was in the form of weapons assistance - assistance, which merely strengthened the Batista dictatorship - assistance which completely failed to advance the economic welfare of the Cuban people - assistance, which enabled Castro and the Communists to encourage the growing belief that America was indifferent to Cuban aspirations for a decent life.

This year Mr. Nixon admitted that if we had formulated a program of Latin American economic development five years ago "It might have produced economic progress in Cuba which might have averted the Castro takeover." But what Mr. Nixon neglects to mention is the fact that he was in Cuba 5 years ago himself - gaining experience. He saw the conditions. He talked with the leaders. He knew what our aid program consisted of. But his only conclusion as stated in a Havana press conference, was his statement that he was "very much impressed with the competence and stability" of the Batista dictatorship.

Mr. Nixon could not see then what should have been obvious - and which should have been even more obvious when he made his ill-fated Latin American trip in 1958 - that unless the Cuban people, with our help, made substantial economic progress, trouble was on its way....

Secondly, in a manner certain to antagonize the Cuban people, we used the influence of our Government to advance the interests of and increase the profits of the private American companies, which dominated the island's economy. At the beginning of 1959 United States companies owned about 40 percent of the Cuban sugar lands - almost all the cattle ranches - 90 percent of the mines and mineral concessions - 80 percent of the utilities - and practically all the oil industry - and supplied two-thirds of Cuba's imports.

The third, and perhaps most disastrous of our failures, was the decision to give stature and support to one of the most bloody and repressive dictatorships in the long history of Latin American repression. Fulgencio Batista murdered 20,000 Cubans in seven years - a greater proportion of the Cuban population than the proportion of Americans who died in both World Wars, and he turned Democratic Cuba into a complete police state - destroying every individual liberty.

Yet our aid to his regime, and the ineptness of our policies, enabled Batista to invoke the name of the United States in support of his reign of terror.

Administration spokesmen publicly praised Batista - hailed him as a staunch ally and a good friend - at a time when Batista was murdering thousands, destroying the last vestiges of freedom, and stealing hundreds of millions of dollars from the Cuban people, and we failed to press for free elections.

In October 1958 - just a few days before Batista held a rigged and fraudulent election - Secretary of State Dulles was the guest of honor at a reception held by the Batista Embassy in Washington. The reception made only the social pages in Washington; but it made the

Havana papers - and it was used by Batista to show how America favored his rule."

JFK could not have stated more eloquently that the rise of Castro was absolutely caused by the ineptitude and absence of foreign policy by the current administrations. The collusion of corporate leaders, politicians and criminals exploited Cuba and its people for pleasure and profits neglecting the basic human needs of the population. The notion that the foreign policy advisors could be taken by surprise by the revolution is a testament to the indifference that was rampant by the American policy makers. In a desperate attempt to put the genie back in the bottle US policy turned to aggression against Cuba.

On December 11, 1959 Chief for the Western Hemisphere Division of the CIA Joseph Caldwell King a vice-president at Johnson and Johnson in charge of Brazil and Argentina and a member of Nelson Rockefeller's Coordinator of Inter-American Affairs (CIAA), sent a cable to Allen Dulles convincing him that Fidel Castro was provoking other Latin American Countries to action against the US. In reaction to the information Dulles created a ZR/Rifle Death squad of mostly Latin Americans which he named OPERATION 40. The Unit was presided over by:

- Vice- President **Richard Nixon**
- **Admiral Arleigh Burke** founder of the Center for Strategic and International Studies (CSIS) another privately funded foreign policy think tank whose board of trustees include Henry Kissinger, Zbigniew Brzezinski, William Cohen, and Brent Scowcroft all directors of the CFR.
- National Security Adviser **Gordon Gray**

- **Allen Dulles**, Director of the CFR from 1927

To head the Cuban task force of Operation 40 Tracy Barnes was appointed CIA Assistant Deputy Director for Plans, under the direction of Richard M. Bissell, Jr. who was also a CFR and Trilateral Commission Member. Barnes set up a meeting in January 1960 in Washington DC with fellow CIA agents that worked together with him before in the 1954 overthrow of Jacobo Arbenz of Guatemala, These included:

- **David Atlee Phillips,** became CIA chief of all operations in the Western hemisphere
- **Jacob Esterline,** CIA station chief in Guatemala, Venezuela and Panama
- **E. Howard Hunt,** plotted the first Watergate burglary, and other undercover operations for the White House that spawned the Watergate Scandal.
- **Frank Bender,** During WWII he worked for the Office of Strategic Services (OSS)
- **David Sanchez Morales ,** instrumental in the CIA's secret war in Laos, the capture of Che Guevara, and the overthrow of Salvador Allende of Chile .

These men recruited mercenaries, former Batiste-regime intelligence officers, assassins and anti-Castro groups as assets for the group. Some of the most infamous members of Operation 40 were

- **Frank Sturgis**, became one of the Watergate burglars.
- **Felix Rodriguez,** became involved in the assassination of Che Guevara, flew 300

helicopter missions in Vietnam, and has numerous ties to George H. W. Bush during the Iran-Contra Affair.

- **Luis Posada Carriles** accused of terrorist activities against Cuba, he is demanded by Venezuela for his key role in the execution of the 1976 Cubana Flight 455 bombing.
- **Orlando Bosch** founder of the Coordination of United Revolutionary Organizations, CORU, accused of taking part with Carriles in terrorist attacks
- **Barry Seal** a United States aircraft pilot turned drug dealer who flew flights for the CIA and the Medellín Drug Cartel during the Iran-Contra era.

In response to pressures from American economic and political interests the CIA was authorized to wage a clandestine war against Marxist Fidel Castro and his communist regime. The operation had to be covert because Soviet intervention was feared would be a result of an all out American military campaign against Cuba. The perceived apparent successes of previous CIA coup's in Iran and Guatemala gave the US government confidence in the ability of the CIA to bring about Castro's demise. On March 17, 1960, US President Dwight D. Eisenhower at a meeting of the US National Security Council (NSC) put in motion the plan propagated by the 5412 Committee:

```
A   PROGRAM   OF   COVERT   ACTION
AGAINST THE CASTRO REGIME:

Objective:
```

The purpose of the program outlined herein is to bring about the replacement of the Castro regime with one more devoted to the true interests of the Cuban people and more acceptable to the U.S. in such a manner to avoid any appearance of U.S. intervention.

Code-named *Operation Pluto* the operation was headed by Richard M. Bissell, Jr., under Allen Dulles. E. Howard Hunt and Gerry Droller began to recruit anti-Castro Cuban exiles in the Miami area while training and military operations were conducted by Jacob Esterline, Col. Jack Hawkins and Colonel Stanley W. Beerli. The invasion began in April 1961 the CIA flew people, supplies, and arms from Florida at night. On April 9, 1961, men, ships, and aircraft started transferring from Guatemala to Puerto Cabezas, Nicaragua. On April 17, 1961, a CIA operated contingency entered the Bay of Pigs on the southern coast of Cuba with a force of transport ships carrying about 1,400 Cuban exile ground troops with tanks and armaments. They were immediately met with Cuban armed forces, trained and equipped by Eastern Bloc nations, who defeated the invading combatants within three days.

In November 1961, CIA inspector general Lyman B Kirkpatrick authored a report 'Survey of the Cuban Operation', at the request of President John F. Kennedy that was declassified in 1996. In response to the findings of this report Allen Dulles, Charles Cabell, and Richard Bissell despite rigorous opposition from the intelligence and military community were forced to resign by early 1962. As for the other members and leaders of Operation 40 they all rose through the ranks of the US intelligent community to become its operatives, assets and leaders in the twentieth century.

Cuba remains one of America's worst performances in foreign policy and as a result the Cuban people for over fifty years have experienced economic paralysis by imposed US sanctions yet trade with China another communist country has no such restrictions. The US suffers a long history of foreign affairs debacles and nearly every foreign relationship is crippled by the covert actions of the CIA and National Security Council. The world sees America as an imperialist threat because they have seen what we have done. The mantra of "Plausible deniability" is nothing but the intelligence community's refusal to deal with or change the policies that have failed for so many years. These policies are influenced by global corporate greed that has no allegiance to the constitutional republic entrusted to us by the Founding Fathers or devotion to humanity beyond their self interest.

Statement of Congressman Ron Paul
United States House of Representatives
What If?
February 12, 2009

What if we wake up one day and realize that the terrorist threat is a predictable consequence of our meddling in the affairs of others?

What if propping up repressive regimes in the Middle East endangers both the United States and Israel?

What if occupying countries like Iraq and Afghanistan – and bombing Pakistan – is directly related to the hatred directed toward us and has nothing to do with being free and prosperous?

What if someday it dawns on us that losing over 5,000 American military personnel in the Middle East since 9/11 is not a fair trade-off for the loss of nearly 3,000 American citizens, no matter how many Iraqi, Pakistani, and Afghan people are killed or displaced?

What if we finally decide that torture, even if called "enhanced interrogation techniques," is self- destructive and produces no useful information – and that contracting it out to a third world nation is just as evil?

What if it is finally realized that war and military spending is always destructive to the economy?

What if all wartime spending is paid for through the deceitful and evil process of inflating and borrowing?

What if we finally see that wartime conditions always undermine personal liberty?

What if conservatives, who preach small government, wake up and realize that our interventionist foreign policy provides the greatest incentive to expand the government?

What if conservatives understood once again that their only logical position is to reject military intervention and managing an empire throughout the world?

What if the American people woke up and understood that the official reasons for going to war are almost always based on lies and promoted by war propaganda in order to serve special interests?

What if we as a nation came to realize that the quest for empire eventually destroys all great nations?

What if Obama has no intention of leaving Iraq?

What if a military draft is being planned for the wars that will spread if our foreign policy is not changed?

What if the American people learn the truth: that our foreign policy has nothing to do with   national security and that it never changes from one administration to the next?

What if war and preparation for war is a racket serving the special interests?

What if President Obama is completely wrong about Afghanistan and it turns out worse than Iraq and Vietnam put together?

What if Christianity actually teaches peace and not preventive wars of aggression?

What if diplomacy is found to be superior to bombs and bribes in protecting America?

What happens if my concerns are completely unfounded – nothing!

According to Daniel Hopsinger this photograph was taken in a nightclub in Mexico City on 22nd January, 1963. The man closest to the camera on the left is Felix Rodriguez, next to him is Porter Goss and Barry Seal. Frank Sturgis is attempting to hide his face with his coat. Albertao 'Loco' Blanco (3rd right) and Jorgo Robreno (4th right).

The following declassified CIA documents are reproduced. (Clearer copies could be found online). As Americans we have the privilege of voting our leaders into the government but with the privileges come the responsibility to make the right choice. This grave responsibility must be met with proper education of the history of this country and the actions of those who have undermined our liberties. These documents prove conclusively that the American public at large has been lied to by the mass media in every instance of foreign and domestic action. The only constant that the American people can rest upon is the Constitution of our government in the form it was given to us by our founding fathers and not the one that has been diluted today. For we cannot believe what we here on television so we must go back and reinstate the principles of liberty that made this country great.

TOP SECRET

C. CONCLUSIONS AND RECOMMENDATIONS

Certain basic conclusions have been drawn from this survey
of the Cuban operation:

1. The Central Intelligence Agency, after starting to
build up the resistance and guerrilla forces inside Cuba,
drastically converted the project into what rapidly became
an overt military operation. The Agency failed to recognize
that when the project advanced beyond the stage of plausible
denial it was going beyond the area of Agency responsibility
as well as Agency capability.

2. The Agency became so wrapped up in the military
operation that it failed to appraise the chances of success
realistically. Furthermore, it failed to keep the national
policy-makers adequately and realistically informed of the
conditions considered essential for success, and it did not
press sufficiently for prompt policy decisions in a fast
moving situation.

3. As the project grew, the Agency reduced the exiled
leaders to the status of puppets, thereby losing the
advantages of their active participation.

4. The Agency failed to build up and supply a resistance
organization under rather favorable conditions. Air and boat
operations showed up poorly.

5. The Agency failed to collect adequate information on the strengths of the Castro regime and the extent of the opposition to it; and it failed to evaluate the available information correctly.

6. The project was badly organized. Command lines and management controls were ineffective and unclear. Senior Staffs of the Agency were not utilized; air support stayed independent of the project; the role of the large forward base was not clear.

7. The project was not staffed throughout with top-quality people, and a number of people were not used to the best advantage.

8. The Agency entered the project without adequate assets in the way of boats, bases, training facilities, agent nets, Spanish-speakers, and similar essential ingredients of a successful operation. Had these been already in being, much time and effort would have been saved.

9. Agency policies and operational plans were never clearly delineated, with the exception of the plan for the brigade landing; but even this provided no disaster plan, no unconventional warfare annex, and only extremely vague plans for action following a successful landing. In general, Agency plans and policies did not precede the

various operations in the project but were drawn up in response to operational needs as they arose. Consequently, the scope of the operation itself and of the support required was constantly shifting.

There were some good things in this project. Much of the support provided was outstanding (for example, logistics and communications). A number of individuals did superior jobs. Many people at all grade levels gave their time and effort without stint, working almost unlimited hours over long periods, under difficult and frustrating conditions, without regard to personal considerations. But this was not enough.

It is assumed that the Agency, because of its experience in this Cuban operation, will never again engage in an operation that is essentially an overt military effort. But before it takes on another major covert political operation it will have to improve its organization and management drastically. It must find a way to set up an actual task force, if necessary, and be able to staff it with the best people. It must govern its operation with clearly defined policies and carefully drawn plans, engaging in full coordination with the Departments of State and Defense as appropriate.

Previous surveys and other papers written by the Inspector General have called attention to many of these problems and deficiencies, and have suggested solutions. For example, in

June 1958 a recommendation was made, in a survey of the Far East
Division, that a high-level Agency study be made of the extent
to which the Agency should be engaged in paramilitary operations,
"if any"; and that it include an evaluation of the capabilities
of other government departments to assume primary responsibility
in this field.

In January 1959 the Inspector General pointed out in a
memorandum to the Deputy Director (Plans) that: "A basic
problem in the PM field is the delineation of responsibility
between the Agency and the military services. In our view, the
Clandestine Services tends to assume responsibilities beyond
its capabilities and does not give sufficient consideration to
the ability of other Departments of the Government to conduct
or participate in these operations."

A 1955 survey of the then Psychological and Paramilitary
Operations Staff warned against the by-passing of this staff
by the operating divisions, who were dealing directly with the
Deputy Director (Plans) and the Director of Central Intelligence
instead. In March 1961 the survey of the Covert Action Staff
again warned against ignoring the staff and failing to utilize
its services.

The July 1959 survey of the Deputy Director (Plans)
organization again stressed the importance of the functional
staffs, particularly in relation to the conduct of complex

operations, and advocated the use of a task force for covert
operations having major international significance.

"These operations", the survey stated, "may be aimed at
the overthrow of a hostile regime and may require extensive
paramilitary operations, ... and clandestine logistics and
air support of substantial magnitude. Such operations must
be coordinated with national policy on a continuing basis,
and may require constant high-level liaison with the State
Department and the White House. To be successful, major covert
operations of this nature require the effective mobilization of
all the resources of the DD/P, and are clearly beyond the
capabilities of any one area division."

The same survey added that the Caribbean task force located
in the WH Division was planning at a great rate, but accomplishing
little because it was too low-level to act decisively or to obtain
effective policy guidance from other departments of the Government;
it did not even inspire confidence among many senior DD/P officers.
Such task forces within a single division "represent a woefully
inadequate response to a problem of major national significance.
Command of such a task force must be a full-time job, and the task
force commander must be of sufficient stature to deal directly
with the Under Secretary of State or with other senior officials
of the government as the need arises."

The same survey also discussed the management problem in the DD/P area at length, and made a number of recommendations which are on record. Among other things, it pointed out the confusion as to the relationship and functions of the three top officers.

The study of the Cuban operation shows that these criticisms and many others discussed in previous Inspector General surveys are still valid and worthy of review. But the Cuban operation, in addition to demonstrating old weaknesses again, also showed Agency weaknesses not clearly discerned before.

The Inspector General, as a result of his study of the Cuban operation, makes the following recommendations regarding future Agency involvement in covert operations which have major international significance and which may profoundly affect the course of world events:

1. Such an operation should be carried out by a carefully selected task force, under the command of a senior official of stature on a full-time basis, and organizationally outside the DD/P structure but drawing upon all the resources of the Clandestine Services.

2. The Agency should request that such projects should be transferred to the Department of Defense when they show signs of becoming overt or beyond Agency capabilities.

3. The Agency should establish a procedure under which the Board of National Estimates or other body similarly divorced from clandestine operations would be required to evaluate all plans for such major covert operations, drawing on all available intelligence and estimating the chances of success from an intelligence point of view.

4. The Agency should establish a high-level board of senior officers from its operational and support components, plus officers detailed from the Pentagon and the Department of State, to make cold, hard appraisals at recurring intervals of the chances of success of major covert projects from an operational point of view.

5. A mechanism should be established for communicating these intelligence and operational appraisals to the makers of national policy.

6. In return, a mechanism should be established to communicate to the Agency the national policy bearing on such projects, and the Agency should not undertake action until clearly defined policy has been received.

7. The Agency should improve its system for the guided collection of information essential to the planning and carrying out of such projects.

8. The Agency should take immediate steps to eliminate the deficiencies in its clandestine air and maritime operations.

9. The Agency should take steps to improve its employees' competence in foreign languages, knowledge of foreign areas, and capability in dealing with foreign people, when such skills are necessary.

10. The Agency should devise a more orderly system for the assignment of employees within the DD/P area than that currently in use.

TELEGRAM
INCOMING

Foreign Service of the
United States of America

SECRET
Classification

ACTION

Control:

Rec'd: APRIL 24, 1961

FROM: SECSTATE WASHINGTON

NO: CIRCR 1662 APRIL 23 6:00 P.M.

NEW DELHI ALSO PASS KATMANDU FROM DEPT.

DEPCIRTEL 1637.

FOL PROVIDED FOR YOUR INFO AND ORAL USE AS NEEDED AS BACK GROUND FOR
HIGHLEVEL OFFICIAL DISCUSSION CUBAN DEVELOPMENTS.

A. VOLUNTEER FORCE OF SOME 1,200 CUBAN FREEDOM FIGHTERS LANDED ON
SOUTH COAST OF CUBA IN EARLY MORNING APRIL 17 FOR DECLARED PURPOSE
LIBERATING THEIR COUNTRY FROM COMMUNIST DICTATORSHIP FIDEL
CASTRO. THEY WERE ALL CUBANS UNDER CUBAN COMMANDER. THEY HAD
RECEIVED SUPPORT FROM AMERICAN SOURCES, BOTH OFFICIAL AND PRIVATE,
AS WELL AS SUPPORT ELSEWHERE IN CLASSICAL MANNER SUCH REFUGEE
EFFORTS. THEY HAD BEEN TRAINING FOR MONTHS AND DEMANDING OPPORTUNITY
TO STRIKE THEIR BLOW FOR FREEDOM. THE TIMING OF THEIR EFFORT WAS DUE
TO THEIR DETERMINATION, THE PROSPECT OF HEAVY MILITARY BUILD-UP
BY CASTRO WITH COMMUNIST SUPPORT, INCLUDING IMMINENT JET CAPABILITY
WITH EXPECTED RETURN CZECH-TRAINED CUBAN PILOTS, AND ONSET OF
RAINY SEASON. ACHIEVEMENT OF PRIMARY OBJECTIVE--OVERTHROW OF CASTRO
REGIME--DEPENDED ON SUBSTANTIAL INTERNAL UPRISINGS AGAINST CASTRO
TO BE STIMULATED BY THEIR ADMITTEDLY LIMITED MILITARY EFFORT.
IT WAS RECOGNIZED THAT, FAILING PROMPT SUPPORT OF SUBSTANTIAL

SECRET
Classification

FORM FS-412P
3-1-58

ᴛELEGRAM
INCOMING

**Foreign Service of the
United States of America**

SECRET
_____
Classification

Control:

Recd: APRIL 24, 1961

CIRCR 1662 CONT'D

SUBSTANTIAL ELEMENTS OF CUBANS IN CUBA, GROUP WOULD NECESSARILY
PASS TO GUERRILLA ACTIVITY. ACTUAL OPERATION BADLY MAULED BY
HEAVY AIR AND TANK ACTIVITY. ALSO TOTALITARIAN CONTROL APPARATUS
WAS FAR MORE EFFECTIVE THAN PREDICTED. AFTER GALLANT EFFORT
BEACHHEAD WAS OVERRUN ON AFTERNOON APRIL 19. SOME FREEDOM FIGHTERS
ARE BELIEVED TO HAVE JOINED GUERRILLAS, SOME WITHDREW, SOME ESCAPED ᴋ
BEACHHEAD IN BOATS, BUT CASUALTIES SEVERE. THE INTIMIDATION AND
MASSIVE ROUNDUP IN CONCENTRATION AREAS OF PERSONS KNOWN TO BE
UNSYMPATHETIC TO CASTRO REGIME, COUPLED WITH FAILURE OF EXPEDITIONARY
FORCE TO STRIKE THROUGH CASTRO'S DEFENSE AND MAKE CONTACT WITH POP-
-ULATION SEVERELY LIMITED POSSIBILITIES OF SPONTANEOUS UPRISING.

RUSK

SECRET
_____
Classification

CS Historical Paper
No. _____ 208 _____

CLANDESTINE SERVICE HISTORY

OVERTHROW OF PREMIER MOSSADEQ OF IRAN

November 1952-August 1953

Date written   : March 1954
Date published: October 1969
Written by   : Dr. Donald N
                   Wilber

S E C R E T

HISTORIAN'S NOTE

This paper, entitled Overthrow of Premier Mossadeq of Iran, was written in March 1954 by Dr. Donald N. Wilber who had played an active role in the operation. The study was written because it seemed desirable to have a record of a major operation prepared while documents were readily at hand and while the memories of the personnel involved in the activity were still fresh. In addition, it was felt advisable to stress certain conclusions reached after the operation had been completed and to embody some of these in the form of recommendations applicable to future, parallel operations.

Documents pertaining to the operation described in this paper are in the Project TPAJAX files which are held by the Iran Branch of the Near East and South Asia Division.

All proper names mentioned in this paper have been checked for accuracy and completeness. A serious effort has been made to supply the first name and middle initial of each individual. The omission of any first names and middle initials indicates that such information could not be located.

Dean L. Dodge
NE Division
Historical Officer
March 1969

S E C R E T

Salvatore Santoro

TABLE OF CONTENTS

APPENDICES

A Initial Operational Plan for TPAJAX, as Cabled
from Nicosia to Headquarters on 1 June 1953

B "London" Draft of the TPAJAX Operational Plan

C Foreign Office Memorandum of 23 July 1953 from
British Ambassador Makins to Under Secretary
of State Smith

D Report on Military Planning Aspect of TPAJAX

E Military Critique - Lessons Learned from TPAJAX
re Military Planning Aspects of Coup d'Etat

SECRET

SECRET

CIA and Guatemala Assassination Proposals 1952-1954

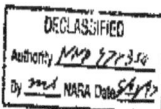

CIA History Staff Analysis

Gerald K. Haines

June 1995

Introduction

In the early 1950s, the Central Intelligence Agency directed covert operations aimed at removing the government of Jacobo Arbenz Guzman from power in Guatemala. Included in these efforts were various suggestions for the disposal of key Arbenz government officials and Guatemalan Communists. The Agency drew up lists of individuals for assassination, discussed training Guatemalan exiles for assassination teams, and conducted intimidation programs against prominent Guatemalan officials.

This brief study traces, in a chronological manner, the injection of assassination planning and proposals into the PBFORTUNE covert operation against the Arbenz government in 1952 and into the PBSUCCESS operation in 1954. It attempts to illustrate the depth of such planning and the level of involvement of Agency officials. It also attempts to detail where the proposals originated, who approved them, and how advanced the preparations for such actions were. Finally, the study examines the implementation of such planning and the results - - i.e., in the end, the plans were abandoned and no Arbenz officials or Guatemalan Communists were killed. The study is based almost exclusively on Directorate of Operations records relating to PBFORTUNE and PBSUCCESS.

Background

As early as 1952 US policymakers viewed the government of President Arbenz with some alarm. Although he had been popularly elected in 1950, growing Communist influence within his government gave rise to concern in the United States that Arbenz had established an effective working alliance with the Communists. Moreover, Arbenz' policies had damaged US business interests in Guatemala; a sweeping agrarian reform called for the expropriation and redistribution of much of the United Fruit Company's land. [1] Although most high-level US officials recognized that a hostile government in Guatemala by itself did not constitute a direct security threat to the United States, they viewed events there in the context of the growing global Cold War struggle with the Soviet Union and feared that Guatemala could become a client state from which the Soviets could project power and influence throughout the Western Hemisphere. [2]

SECRET

—SECRET—

CIA and Intelligence Community reports tended to support the view that Guatemala and the Arbenz regime were rapidly falling under the sway of the Communists.[1] Director of Central Intelligence (DCI) Walter Bedell Smith and other Agency officials believed the situation called for action. Their assessment was, that without help, the Guatemalan opposition would remain inept, disorganized and ineffective. The anti-Communist elements - - the Catholic hierarchy, landowners, business interests, the railway workers union, university students, and the Army were prepared to prevent a Communist accession to power, but they had little outside support.[ ]

Other US officials, especially in the Department of State, urged a more cautious approach. The Bureau of Inter-American Affairs, for example, did not want to present "the spectacle of the elephant shaking with alarm before the mouse.". It wanted a policy of firm persuasion with the withholding of virtually all cooperative assistance, and the concluding of military defense assistance pacts with El Salvador, Nicaragua, and Honduras.[ ] Although the Department of State position became the official public US policy, the CIA assessment of the situation had support within the Truman administration as well. This led to the development of a covert action program designed to topple the Arbenz government - - PBFORTUNE.

PBFORTUNE

Following a visit to Washington by Nicaraguan President Anastasio Somoza in April 1952, in which Somoza boasted that if provided arms he and Guatemalan exile Carlos Castillo Armas could overthrow Arbenz, President Harry Truman asked DCI Smith, to investigate the possibility. Smith sent an agent, codenamed SEEKFORD, to contact Guatemalan dissidents about armed action against the Arbenz regime.[ ] After seeing his report, [ ] Chief of the [ ] Division of the Directorate of Plans (DP), proposed to Deputy Director of Central Intelligence Allen Dulles that the Agency supply Castillo Armas with arms and $225,000 and that Nicaragua and Honduras furnish the Guatemalans with air support.[ ] Gaining Department of State support, Smith, on 9 September 1952, officially approved [ ]'s request to initiate operation PBFORTUNE to aid Guatemalan exiles in overthrowing Arbenz. Planning for PBFORTUNE lasted barely a month, however, when Smith terminated it after he learned in October that it had been blown.[ ]

Throughout planning for PBFORTUNE there were proposals for assassination. Even months before the official approval of PBFORTUNE, Directorate of Plans (DP) officers compiled a "hit list." Working from an old 1949 Guatemalan Army list of Communists and information supplied by the Directorate of Intelligence, in January 1952 DP officers compiled a list of "top flight Communists whom the new government would desire to eliminate immediately in event of successful anti-Communist coup." Headquarters asked [ ] to verify the list and recommend any additions or deletions.[ ] Headquarters also requested [ ] to verify a list of an additional 16 Communists and/or sympathizers whom the new government would desire to incarcerate immediately if the coup succeeded.[ ] [ ] in Guatemala City added three names to the list in his reply.[ ] Nine months later,

SECRET

SEEKFORD, the CIA agent in touch with Castillo Armas, forwarded to Headquarters a disposal list compiled by Castillo Armas. That list called for the execution through executive action of 58 Guatemalans (Category I) and the imprisonment or exile of 74 additional Guatemalans (Category II).[12] SEEKFORD also reported at the same time, 18 September 1952, that General Rafael Trujillo, the dictator of the Dominican Republic, had agreed to aid Castillo Armas in return for the "killing of four Santo Dominicans at present residing in Guatemala a few days prior to D-Day." According to SEEKFORD, Castillo Armas readily agreed, but cautioned that it could not be done prior to D-day because of security reasons. Castillo Armas further added that his own plans included similar action and that special squads were already being trained.[14] There is no record that Headquarters took any action regarding Castillo Armas' list.

After the PBFORTUNE operation was officially terminated, the Agency continued to pick up reports of assassination planning on the part of the Guatemalan opposition. In late November 1952, for example, an opposition Guatemalan leader, in a conversation with SEEKFORD, confirmed that Castillo Armas had special "K" groups whose mission was to kill all leading political and military leaders, and that the hit list with the location of the homes and offices of all targets had already been drawn up.[15] On 12 December SEEKFORD reported further that Castillo Armas planned to make maximum use of the "K" groups.[16] Another source subsequently reported that Nicaraguan, Honduran, and Salvadoran soldiers in civilian clothes would infiltrate Guatemala and assassinate unnamed Communist leaders.[17]

In addition to monitoring events in Guatemala, the Agency continued to try to influence developments and to float ideas for disposing of key figures in the [   ] government. [   ] in 1953 proposed not only to focus on sabotage, defection, penetration, and propaganda efforts with regard to Guatemala, but to eliminate [   ] [   ] According to [   ]'s draft memorandum, after creating a story that [   ] was preparing to oust the Communists, he could be eliminated. His assassination would be "laid to the Commies" and used to bring about a mass defection of the Guatemalan army.[18] A Western Hemisphere Division memo of 28 August 1953 also suggested possibly assassinating key Guatemalan military officers if they refused to be converted to the rebel cause.[19] In September 1953 [   ] also sent [   ] an updated plan of action which included a reference to "neutralizing" key Guatemalan military leaders.[20]

In the psychological warfare area, Guatemala City Station sent [   ] all leading Communists in Guatemala, "death notice" cards for 30 straight days beginning 15 April 1953. The Station repeated the operation beginning 15 June 1953 but reported no reaction from the targeted leaders.[21]

PBSUCCESS

By the fall of 1953, US policymakers, including CIA officials, were searching for a new overall program for dealing with Arbenz. The Guatemalan leader had moved even closer to the Communists. He had expropriated additional United Fruit Company holdings, legalized the Guatemalan Communist Party, the PGT, and suppressed anti-Communist opposition following an abortive uprising at Salamá. In response, the National Security Council authorized a covert action operation against Arbenz and gave the CIA primary responsibility.[21]

·The CIA plan, as drawn up by [   ]s Western Hemisphere Division, combined psychological warfare, economic, diplomatic, and paramilitary actions against Guatemala. Named PBSUCCESS, and coordinated with the Department of State, the plan's stated objective was "to remove covertly, and without bloodshed if possible, the menace of the present Communist-controlled government of Guatemala." In the outline of the operation the sixth stage called for the "roll-up" of Communists and collaborators after a successful coup.[22]

Dulles placed [   ] in charge of PBSUCCESS and sent a senior DDP · officer, [   ] to establish a temporary station (LINCOLN), to coordinate the planning and execution of PBSUCCESS. Other key Agency figures involved were [   ] and [   ]Chief of the[   ] Staff. Department of State [   ] Assistant Secretary of State for [   ] from the Office of [   ] Affairs, and [   ] State liaison to the Agency, also played major roles.

Training

Although assassination was not mentioned specifically in the overall plan, the Chief of [   ]at [   ]requested a special paper on liquidation of personnel on 5 January 1954. This paper, according to the [   ]chief, was to be utilized to brief the training chief for PBSUCCESS before he left to begin training Castillo Armas' forces in Honduras on 10 January 1954. A cable from [   ] the following day requested 20 silencers (converters) for .22 caliber rifles. Headquarters sent the rifles.[24] The [   ]chief also discussed the training plan with the agent SEEKFORD on 13 January 1954, indicating that he wanted Castillo Armas and the PBSUCCESS [   ]officer to train two assassins. In addition, he discussed these "assassination specialists" with Castillo Armas on 3 February 1954.[25]

The idea of forming assassination teams ("K" groups) apparently originated with Castillo Armas in 1952. Adapting Castillo Armas' concept, the [   ]chief routinely included two assassination specialists in his training plans.[26]

CIA planning for sabotage teams in early 1954 also included creating a "K" group trained to perform assassinations. The main mission of the sabotage teams or harassment teams, however, was to attack local Communists and Communist property and to avoid attacks on the army.[27] A chart depicting the [   ] chief's plan for the CALLIGERIS (Castillo Armas) organization showed the "K" Group. It was distributed in various paramilitary planning packets as late as the spring of 1954.[28] In a briefing for [   ] in June 1954, [   ] also mentioned that sabotage teams would assassinate known Communists in their areas once the invasion operation began.[29]

Psychological Warfare

As in PBFORTUNE, an intensive psychological warfare program paralleled the planning for paramilitary action. Utilizing the anti-Communist network established by a Guatemalan dissident, the Chief of Political and Psychological Operations at LINCOLN developed a major propaganda campaign against the Arbenz government. Part of this program included the sending of new mourning cards to top Communist leaders. These cards mourned the imminent purge or execution of various Communists throughout the world and hinted of the forthcoming doom of the addressee. Death letters were also sent to top Guatemalan Communists such as [   ] Guatemala City Station, [   ] prepared these letters for the dissident leader. The "Nerve War Against Individuals," as it was called, also included sending wooden coffins, hangman's nooses, and phony bombs to selected individuals. Such slogans as "Here Lives a Spy" and "You have Only 5 Days" were painted on their houses.[30]

Wanting to go beyond mere threats, the dissident leader suggested that the "violent disposal" of one of the top Guatemalan Communists would have a positive effect on the resistance movement and undermine Communist morale. The dissident leader's recommendations called for the formation of a covert action group to perform violent, illegal acts against the government. LINCOLN cautioned the dissident leader, however, that such techniques were designed only to destroy a person's usefulness. By destroy "we do not mean to kill the man," LINCOLN cabled the dissident leader. Responding to the proposal that a top Communist leader be killed, [   ] Guatemala City told [   ] he could not recommend assassinating any "death letter" recipients at this time because it might touch off "wholesale reprisals." Reiterating that the plan was "to scare not kill," he nevertheless suggested that [   ] might wish to "study the suggestion for utility now or in the future."[31]

While Agency paramilitary and psychological warfare planning both included suggestions which implied assassination proposals, these proposals appear never to have been implemented. The [   ] chief had sought to use Castillo Armas' "K" group scheme but there was no State Department or White House support. Such was also the case when the subject of assassination emerged in high-level Agency and inter-agency planning discussions.

SECRET

Target Lists

A weekly PBSUCCESS meeting at Headquarters on 9 March 1954 considered the elimination of 15-20 of Guatemala's top leaders with "Trujillo's trained pistoleros." Those attending the meeting were [   ]
[   ] DP Operations, along with State Department representatives [   ].
Addressing the group, [   ] while stating clearly that "such elimination was part of the plan and could be done," objected to the proposal at that time. [   ] however, expressed the view that "knocking off" the leaders might make it possible for the Army to take over."[12]

Following this meeting, [   ] appears to be the Agency official who revived discussion of assassination as an option. On 25 March he broached the subject with [   ] who had just returned from the Organization of American States meeting in Caracas, Venezuela, that voted 17 to 1 to condemn communism in Guatemala. With [   ] and [.] again present [   ] asked [   ] if he had changed his thinking since the conference on the possible methods to get rid of the Arbenz government. [   ] replied that in his opinion "the elimination of those in high positions of the government would bring about its collapse." He then qualified his statement, according to [   ]s memo, by saying that perhaps "even a smaller number, say 20, would be sufficient."[13]

Less than a week later [   ] visited [   ] on 31 March. The records do not indicate why [   ] flew to [   ],[14] but on that date the [   ] officers were asked to draw up an up-dated target list. Criteria for inclusion on the disposal list required that individuals be (1) high government and organizational leaders "irrevocably implicated in Communist doctrine and policy," (2) "out and out proven Communist leaders," or (3) those few individuals in key government and military positions of tactical importance "whose removal for psychological, organizational or other reasons is mandatory for the success of military action."[15]

The [   ] chief took the new list with him when he consulted Castillo Armas on 7 April 1954. [   ] also borrowed a copy of the list on the same day. The [   ] chief and Castillo Armas apparently discussed the list and at least tentatively agreed that any assassination would take place during the actual invasion of Guatemala by Castillo Armas' forces. There was still no time date for the actual beginning of hostilities, however.[14]

Agency contacts with conservative Guatemalan exile leader [   ]
[   ] at the same time also produced an assassination list. [   ]
provided a CIA cutout with a list of Communist leaders he would like to see executed.
[   ] saw [   ] as a loose cannon, however. They did not want him to become involved in PBSUCCESS."[15]

CIA received further Department of State encouragement for assassination plotting in April 1954. Fueling the fire for action, [   ] in a meeting with [   ] and another CIA officer, concluded that "more drastic and definitive steps to overthrow the government [in

6

SECRET

Guatemala] must be taken." In response to a question of whether Guatemalan [
       ] was "salvageable," [   ] replied in the negative and
suggested "he be eliminated."[?]

On 16 May 1954 the [   ] Officer at [   ] proposed in a memorandum
to [   ] the new Chief of [   ] and [   ] now serving as [   ]
that assassination be incorporated into the psychological part of PBSUCCESS. The
[   ] Officer laid out a specific assassination schedule leading up to D-Day, the actual
invasion by Castillo Armas. He proposed a raid on [
    ] on D12. This was to be a show of force; no one was to be harmed and the attack
was to take place when [   ] was absent [   ] The [   ] Officer,
however, proposed the disposal of [   ], on
D-10 as a means of paralyzing the [
    ] Th.[   ] Officer suggested that [
    ] be killed on D-8. This would, according to the [   ] Officer, eliminate
the [   ] character of the Arbenz regime. The [   ] Officer called for the
disposal on D-6 of [   ] in the Guatemalan
Communist Party (PGT) [   ] This would
leave Guatemala's [   ] er believed. On
D-4 [   ] would
be eliminated. [   ] was to be eliminated so that the rebel
forces would not have to worry about him or deal with him after victory. The [   ]
Officer considered the possibility of reprisals as a weakness in his scheme, but decided that
"such actions were expected anyway." The [   ] Officer argued that his proposal, if
adopted, would not only be physically impressive but psychologically significant by
providing a show of strength for the opposition. It would also "soften up" the enemy. He
added that his first three suggestions had the previous approval of [   ]."[?]

On 21 May [   ] asked Headquarters for permission to implement the [   ]
Officer's proposal and asked for suggestions about the specific individuals to be
targeted.[40] No reply from Headquarters to [   ] has been found. On 29 May 1954,
however, the [   ] chief requested the names of the "four men" he and the
[   ] Officer discussed assassinating. More than likely, the [   ] chief wanted
to take up the issue again with Castillo Armas. Again, no cable reply from Headquarters
or [   ] has been found.[41] At the same time, [   ] continued compiling
information on [   ] and lists of home addresses for individuals named on the
"disposal list" drafted in April.[42] [   ] believed [   ] was a "worthy target."[43]

Meanwhile, [   ] traveled to Washington and submitted a proposal on 1 June
1954 that suggested that as an alternative approach to the paramilitary action program "
specific sabotage and possibly political assassination should be carefully worked out and
effected."[44] [   ] took up [   ] suggestion in discussions with [   ]
on 1 and 2 June. According to [   ] considered the proposal and then ruled it
out, "at least for the immediate future," on the ground that it would prove counterproductive. [   ] wanted more specific plans concerning the individual targets, timing,
and statement of purpose. Both [   ] and [   ] agreed that the advantages gained
by this type of activity needed to be clearly spelled out.[45] This appears to be the end of

7

SECRET

serious planning in Washington for the inclusion of selective assassination proposals in PBSUCCESS. Returning from Washington to [   ], on 2 June 1954, [   ] however, reported to his staff that the consensus in Washington was that "Arbenz must go; how does not matter."[45]

The Paramilitary Operation

On 16 June 1954 Castillo Armas' CIA-supported force of armed exiles entered Guatemala. While these forces advanced tentatively in the hinterland,[   ]Guatemala City on 16 and 17 June met with a leading Guatemalan military commander, in the hopes of convincing him to lead a coup against Arbenz. In these discussions, the military commander hinted he would like to see [   ], killed. The[   ] frustrated by the continued inaction of the Guatemalan military commander, told him that if he wanted them killed he should do it himself. Despite the Guatemalan military commander's vacillation, a [   ]cable indicated that he remained convinced that [   ]had to be eliminated.[47]

With the Guatemala Army's position uncertain and the outcome still in doubt, a few days later, the [   ]chief, in [   ], requested permission to bomb the [   ]and[   ] LINCOLN responded on 22 June that it did not want to waste air strikes on[   ]or[   ]while a battle was raging at Zacapa.[48] The [   ]and[   ] also supported the[   ]chief's request to bomb[   ] with a dramatic cable which ended "Bomb Repeat Bomb."[49] LINCOLN and Headquarters held fast and[   ] was never bombed. "We do not take action with grave foreign policy implications except as agent for the policymakers," Dulles cabled LINCOLN.[50]

President Arbenz, on 27 June 1954, in a bitterly anti-American speech, resigned his office and sought asylum in the Mexican embassy in Guatemala City. [   ].[51] After Castillo Armas assumed the presidency, however, Arbenz was allowed to leave the country for Mexico, which granted him political asylum. In addition, 120 other Arbenz government officials or Communists departed Guatemala under a safe passage agreement with the Castillo Armas government.[52] There is no evidence that any Guatemalans were executed.

CONCLUSION

CIA officers responsible for planning and implementing covert action against the Arbenz government engaged in extensive discussions over a two-and a half year period about the possibility of assassinating Guatemalan officials [   ] Consideration of using assassination to [   ] purge Guatemala of Communist influence was born of the extreme international tensions in the early Cold War years. The Agency did not act unilaterally, but consulted with State Department officials with responsibility for policy toward Latin America. In the end, no assassinations of Guatemalan officials were carried out, according to all available evidence.

8

SECRET

THE NATIONAL ARCHIVES

. Proposals for assassination pervaded both PBFORTUNE and PBSUCCESS, rather than being confined to an early stage of these programs. Even before official approval of PBFORTUNE, CIA officers compiled elimination lists and discussed the concept of assassination with Guatemalan opposition leaders. Until the day that Arbenz resigned in June 1954 the option of assassination was still being considered.

Discussions of assassination reached a high level within the Agency. Among those involved were [

] is known to have been present at one meeting where the subject of assassination came up. It is likely that [   ] was also aware in general terms that assassination was under discussion. Beyond planning, some actual preparations were made. Some assassins were selected, training began, and tentative "hit lists" were drawn up.

Yet no covert action plan involving assassinations of Guatemalans was ever approved or implemented. The official objective of PBSUCCESS was to remove the Guatemalan government covertly "without bloodshed if possible." Elimination lists were never finalized, assassination proposals remained controversial within the Agency, and it appears that no Guatemalans associated with Arbenz were assassinated. Both CIA and State Department officers were divided (and undecided) about using assassination.

Discussion of whether to assassinate Guatemalan Communists and leaders sympathetic to Communist programs took place in a historical era quite different from the present. Soviet Communism had earned a reputation of using whatever means were expedient to advance Moscow's interests internationally. Considering Moscow's machinations in Eastern Europe, role in the Korean War, sponsorship of subversion through Communist surrogates in the Third World, and espousal of an ideology that seemed to have global hegemony as the ultimate objective, American officials and the American public alike regarded foreign Communist Parties as Soviet pawns and as threatening to vital US security interests.

Cold War realities and perceptions conditioned American attitudes toward what political weapons were legitimate to use in the struggle against Communism. It would be over two decades after the events in Guatemala before DCI William Colby prohibited any CIA involvement in assassination and a subsequent Executive Order banned any US government involvement in assassination.

[1] See Piero Gleijeses, *Shattered Hope: The Guatemalan Revolution and the United States, 1944-1954* (Princeton: Princeton University Press, 1991), pp. 187-88. United Fruit dominated Guatemalan banana production, controlled the International Railroad of Central America, and its merchant fleet had a virtual monopoly of Guatemalan overseas shipping. It was second only to the Guatemalan government as an employer.

[2] See Gleijeses, *Shattered Hope* and Richard H. Immerman, *The CIA in Guatemala: The Foreign Policy of Intervention*, (Austin: University of Texas Press, 1982) for general overviews of the Guatemalan situation in the early 1950s and US reaction. See also John Peurifoy US Ambassador to Guatemala statement of 23 October 1953 in Department of State, *Foreign Relations of the United States, The American Republic 1950-1954*, 4:1093. (Hereinafter cited as FRUS).

[3] See PBSUCCESS Planning Documents, Directorate of Operations, Latin American Division Records, Job Number 79-101025A, CIA Archives (S). See also NSC 144/1, 18 March 1953, FRUS 4: 1-79 and J. C. King, memo for DDP, "Estimate of Situation in Guatemala," 11 January 1952 printed in Michael Warner, ed. *The CIA under Harry Truman* (Washington, DC: Center for the Study of Intelligence, CIA, 1994), pp. 452-53.

[4] J. C. King, Chief, Western Hemisphere Division, dispatch, 22 March 1952, Box 7 (S).

[5] See Bureau of Inter-American Affairs, "Alternative Policy Lines, 1953," and NSC, "Guatemala," 19 August 1953, FRUS, 4:1074-1086.

[6] See cable to Dulles, "Conference with ...," 4 August 1952, Box 69 (S).

[7] See memorandum to Dulles, "Guatemalan Situation," 9 July 1952, Box 67 (S) and memorandum to Dulles, "Conference with ...," 4 August 1952, Box 69 (S).

[8] See [   ]"Chronology of Meeting's Leading to Approval of Project A," 8 October 1952, Box 69 (S); to [   ] "Guatemala," 8 October 1952, Box 69 (S); and to Dulles, "Guatemala Situation," 9 July 1952, Box 69.

[9] See [   ]"Chronology of Meetings Leading to Approval of Project A." (S). See also Immerman, *CIA in Guatemala*, pp. 120-22. Because of security leaks and the boasting of General Somoza about his and the Agency's role in supporting the rebellion PBFORTUNE was soon called off. Secretary of State Dean Acheson asked DCI Smith to stop the operation on October 1952.

[10] See Cable 24629 OPC/OSO/WHD to [   ] 26 January 1952, Box 7 (S). For a list of the names and biographical data see, Chief, Economic Warfare Operations, LINCOLN to All Staff Officers, "Selection of Individuals for Disposal by Junta Group," 31 March 1954, Box 145.

[11] Washington Cable [   ] to [   ] 29 January 1952, Box 7 (S).

[12] [   ] to Headquarters, 29 January 1952, Box 10 (S).

[13] See to [   ] "Guatemala Communist Personnel to be Disposed of During Military Operations of CALLIGERIS," (Castillo Armas), 18 September 1952, Box 134 (S).

[14] See, Report # 3 to [   ] "Liaison between CALLEGERIS and General Trujillo of Santo Domingo," 18 September 1952, Box 134 (S). Assassination was a nasty but frequent tool of Guatemalan politics. Arbenz himself benefited from the killing of his arch rival for the presidency Francisco Arana in 1949.

[15] See to [   ] memo, "Conference," 1 December 1952, Box 134 (S).

[16] "To [   ] memo, "Current Planning of Calligeris Organization," 12 December 1952, Box 134 (S). See also, Acting Chief, [   ] Branch, Western Hemisphere Division that reported in November 1952 that Castillo Armas was studying PW use of liquidation lists. Memorandum for the record, "PW Conference," 5 November 1952, Box 151 (S). The case officer also reported that the Arbenz government had targeted Castillo Armas for assassination.

[17] See [   ] 10 March 1953, Box 150 (S).

[18] See [   ] memorandum, "Proposed Course of Action If Plan is Not Continued in Present Form," undated but probably 1953, Box 134 (S).

[19] Western Hemisphere Division, memo, "PBFORTUNE," 28 August 1953, Box 72 (S).

[20] See [   ] memo to [   ] "Guatemala - General Plan of Action," 11 September 1953, Box 5 (TS). See also the attached memorandum from [   ] to [   ] 9 September 1953 (TS).

SECRET

" See Dispatch, COS Guatemala City to LINCOLN, "Death Notices," 19 April 1954, Box 99 (S).
" NSC Policy Paper, 19 August 1953, FRUS 4:1081.
" See [ ] to [ ] "Guatemala - General Plan of Action," Box 5 (TS) and [ ]
Special Deputy for PBSUCCESS, memo for the record, "Program for PBSUCCESS," 12 November 1953,
Box 135 (C). See also, memo to [ ] "Summary of Directives and Instructions on PBSUCCESS," 5
November 1953, Box 142 (S). [ ] does not specially mention assassination either.
" [ ] opened on 9 December. See [ ] to Headquarters, 5 January
1954, Box 1 (S) and [ ] to Headquarters 6 January 1954, Box 1 (S). See also 38 to
Headquarters, 9 March 1954, Box 13 (S); [ ] to Headquarters, 4 January 1954, Box 1 (S);.
" See the [ ] chief to Chief, [ ]. "CALLIGERIS Briefing Notes," 1
February 1954 , Box 147 (S). See also, Chief, [ ] memo for
[ ] "Cost of Support for PBSUCCESS," 27 September 1954, Box 43 (S). He listed the 20 silenced
rifles. See also [ ] to Headquarters, 6 January 1954, Box 75 (S) and [ ] 2 to
Headquarters, 21 January 1954, Box 1 (S).
" To [ ] Report #5, [ ]. " 18 September 1953, Box 73 (S) and
[ ] chief, memo for the record, "PM Conference Held at [ ] " 13 February 1954, Box 74
(S). See also [ ] to Headquarters, 4 January 1954, Box 1 (S). The Headquarters Registry copy
of the pouch manifest for, 8 January 1954, Box 97 (S) lists the manual "A Study of Assassination." A
handwritten note on the original manifest says the pouch was carried to [ ] by [ ]. The actual
assassination study is in Box 145 (S).
" See [ ] to Headquarters, 8 June 1954, Box 5 (S) or [ ] to
Headquarters, 8 June 1954, Box 5 (S).
" See it [ ] Report # 22, "Current Planning of CALLIGERIS Organization," 12 December
1952, Box 136 (S) and "Contact Report," 13 January 1954, (S).
" See Dispatch, to [ ]. "Training," 6 June 1954, Box 75
(Secret, PBSUCCESS, Rybat). [ ]

" To LINCOLN, 16 May 1954, "Tactical Instructions (part II)," (S) and To LINCOLN,
"Instructions' Nerve War Against Individuals," 9 June 1954, Box 50 (S).
" See COS Guatemala City, to Western Hemisphere Division, undated, Box 46, (C) and
Guatemala City 553 to LINCOLN, 14 May 1954. See also the COS, dispatch Guatemala City to
LINCOLN, 14 May 1954, Box 145 (S). [ ]

" See [ ] memo for the record, "Weekly PBSUCCESS Meeting with [ ] " 9 March 1954,
Box 156 (TS). Even before this meeting [ ] suggested that the top Guatemalan leadership
needed to be assassinated during the first hours of the revolution. They had to be "pulled out by the
roots." If we waited [ ] argued, "if too many of these birds get out they will be back in about
three years." See [ ] Tape 17, Box 209 (S). [ ]

[ ] "Administrative Details," 13 April 1954, Box 70 (S); [ ] memo for the record, "Meeting." 2
March 1954, Box 70 (S).
" [ ] memo for the record, "Report of Mr. [ ] on OAS Conference," 29 March
1954, Box 145 (TS).
" See, Chief, Economic Warfare, [ ] memo to All Staff Officers, "Selection of
Individuals for Disposal by Junta Group," 31 March 1954, Box 145 (S). We know [ ] visited
[ ] on this date from the [ ] visitors log book. He signed into [ ] on 31 March.
See [ ] Log Book for 31 March 1954, Box 138 (S).
" Memo, Box 145 (S).
" See memo and attachment notes on the memo which indicates that [ ] returned the list to
the file on 1 June 1954, Box 145 (S)
" [ ]

[ ]

11

SECRET

1950. See memo to [   ] "Summary of Operation," 18 April 1954, Box 134 (S). See also Dispatch,
[   ] to [   ] "Assets in Guatemala," 14 April 1954, Box 134 (S). An attachment notes that some
assets are also on another list for "eradication." (see attachment in Box 102). See also [   ] to
[   ] 5 April 1954, Box 125 (S).

⁴⁴ See memo for the record, "Synthesis of [   ]'s remarks Relevant to
PBSUCCESS Made at a Meeting 21 April 1954," 22 April 1954, Box 151 (S).

⁴⁵ See [   ] Officer, [   ] and [   ]. "Acts of Force Before D-Day,"
16 May 1954, Box 142 (Secret, PBSUCCESS, Rybat). See also [   ] memo to [   ] Officer,
undated, in which [   ] states, "Your views were discussed with Chief, [   ]" Box 145 (Secret,
PBSUCCESS, Rybat).

⁴⁶ See [   ] to Director, 21 May 1954, Box 4 (S) and [   ] to Director, 21
May 1954, Box 4 (S).

⁴⁷ See to Headquarters, 29 May 1954, Box 13 (S). Perhaps [   ] Officer, [   ] and
[   ] "Contact
chief [   ] talked at a conference held at [   ] on 2 June 1954. See [   ]"
Report," 2 June 1954, Box 146 (Secret, PBSUCCESS, Rybat).

⁴⁸ See dispatch, [   ] to [   ] "X-Program, [   ]" 25 May 1954, Box
145 (Secret, PBSUCCESS, Rybat).

⁴⁹ See "Disposal List Home Addresses," copied from an attachment to dispatch, [   ]
[   ] to [   ] 1 June 1954, Box 145, (S). It contained 15 names. See also [   ] routing slip
for the attachment. (Dispatch dated 25 May 1954), Box 145 (Secret, Rybat).

⁵⁰ See [   ] draft memo, "Present Status and Possible Future Course of PBSUCCESS," 1 June
1954, Box 145 (S).

⁵¹ [   ] memo for the record, "Points Covered in H/W Discussions of June 1 and 2," 3 June
1954, Box 145, (S). This memo is originally from Job 00075R, Box 1, Folder 3.

⁵² See "Contact Report," 2 June 1954, Box 146 (Secret, PBSUCCESS, Rybat). See also [   ]
memo for the record, "Points Covered in H/W Discussion of June 1 and 2," 3 June 1954 and [   ]
note for the file, "Disposal List Prepared by C/EW," 1 June 1954, Box 145 (S).

⁵³ See [   ] to Headquarters, 17 June 1954, Box 75 (S); [   ] to
Headquarters, 18 June 1954, Box 11 (S). See earlier Agency meetings with Guatemalan military leader,
"First Meeting, 4 May 1954, Dispatch, [   ] to [   ] 1 June 1954, Box 134 (S);
Dispatch, 11 June 1954, Box 134 (S); and Dispatch, [   ] to [   ], 4 May 1954, Box 154
(S). For [   ]'s cable, see [   ] to [   ], 24 June 1954, Box 153 (Secret,
PBSUCCESS, Rybat).

⁵⁴ See [   ] to LINCOLN, 14 June 1954, Box 93 (Secret, PBSUCCESS, Rybat);
[   ] to LINCOLN, 19 June 1954, Box 93 (S); and LINCOLN, 4175 to Headquarters, 22
June 1954, Box 93 (Secret, PBSUCCESS, Rybat).

⁵⁵ [   ] to LINCOLN, 25 June 1954, Box 146 (S) and [   ] to
Dulles, 19 June 1954, Box 91 (S).

⁵⁶ See Headquarters to LINCOLN, 5857, 22 June 1954, Box 143, (TS).

⁵⁷ See Guatemala City 977 to LINCOLN, 27 June 1954, Box 145 (Secret, PBSUCCESS, Rybat).

⁵⁸ John K. Waller, CIA Inspector General, letter to Thomas Farmer, Chairman of the Intelligence
Oversight Board, 15 October 1979.

Chapter 9

"JFK and his speech to the press"

"The very word "secrecy" is repugnant in a free and open society; and we are as a people inherently and historically opposed to secret societies, to secret oaths and secret proceedings. We decided long ago that the dangers of excessive and unwarranted concealment of pertinent facts far outweighed the dangers which are cited to justify it. Even today, there is little value in opposing the threat of a closed society by imitating its

arbitrary restrictions. Even today, there is little value in insuring the survival of our nation if our traditions do not survive with it. And there is very grave danger that an announced need for increased security will be seized upon those anxious to expand its meaning to the very limits of official censorship and concealment. That I do not intend to permit to the extent that it is in my control. And no official of my Administration, whether his rank is high or low, civilian or military, should interpret my words here tonight as an excuse to censor the news, to stifle dissent, to cover up our mistakes or to withhold from the press and the public the facts they deserve to know."

"For we are opposed around the world by a monolithic and ruthless conspiracy that relies on covert means for expanding its sphere of influence--on infiltration instead of invasion, on subversion instead of elections, on intimidation instead of free choice, on guerrillas by night instead of armies by day. It is a system which has conscripted vast human and material resources into the building of a tightly knit, highly efficient machine that combines military, diplomatic, intelligence, economic, scientific and political operations.

Its preparations are concealed, not published. Its mistakes are buried not headlined. Its dissenters are silenced, not praised. No expenditure is questioned, no rumor is printed, no secret is revealed."

"No President should fear public scrutiny of his

program. For from that scrutiny comes understanding; and from that understanding comes support or opposition. And both are necessary. I am not asking your newspapers to support the Administration, but I am asking your help in the tremendous task of informing and alerting the American people. For I have complete confidence in the response and dedication of our citizens whenever they are fully informed.

I not only could not stifle controversy among your readers-- I welcome it. This Administration intends to be candid about its errors; for as a wise man once said: "An error does not become a mistake until you refuse to correct it." We intend to accept full responsibility for our errors; and we expect you to point them out when we   miss   them.

Without debate, without criticism, no Administration and no country can succeed-- and no republic can survive. That is why the Athenian lawmaker Solon decreed it a crime for any citizen to shrink from controversy. And that is why our press was protected by the First Amendment-- the only business in America specifically protected by the Constitution-- not primarily to amuse and entertain, not to emphasize the trivial and sentimental, not to simply "give the public what it wants"--but to inform, to arouse, to reflect, to state our dangers and our opportunities, to indicate our crises and our choices, to lead, mold educate and sometimes even anger public opinion.

This means greater coverage and analysis of international news-- for it is no longer far away and foreign but close at hand and local. It means greater attention to improved understanding of the news as well as improved transmission. And it means, finally, that government at all levels, must meet its obligation to provide you with the fullest possible information outside the narrowest limits of national security...

"And so it is to the printing press--to the recorder of mans deeds, the keeper of his conscience, the courier of his news-- that we look for strength and assistance, confident that with your help man will be what he was born to be: free and independent."

John Fitzgerald Kennedy
April 27, 1961

The speech that President John F. Kennedy gave at the Waldorf-Astoria Hotel before the American Newspaper Publishers Association was a plea to the press to not censure the news and that government was obliged to tell the truth. *"And it means, finally, that government at all levels, must meet its obligation to provide you with the fullest possible information outside the narrowest limits of national security..."* This was an impossible scenario as the propaganda machine of the twentieth century has always been since its inception controlled by a very small group of corporations in a closely knit association of members. The battle for the minds of men and their vote is a front that the elite take exceedingly serious, public sentiment is the key to a successful global doctrine. Truth is sacrificed on the altar of the information war and it is replaced by a controlled agenda.

As far back as 1915 investigations have determined that the News Papers were being purchased to control public opinion. This was revealed in an investigation by Francis Oscar Callaway a three term U.S. Representative from Texas twelfth district from 1911 to 1917 his findings were published in the **Congressional Record** the official record of the proceedings and debates of the United States Congress. It is published by the United States Government Printing Office, and is issued daily when the United States Congress is in session. These findings were published in volume 54 of February 9, 1917 page 2947 and state:

"In March 1915 the JP Morgan interests the steel shipbuilding and powder interests and their subsidiary organizations got together 12 men high up in the newspaper world and employed them to select the most influential newspapers in the United States and sufficient number of them to control generally the policy of the daily press of the United States.

These 12 men worked the problem out by selecting 179 newspapers and then began by an elimination process to retain only those necessary for the purpose of controlling the general policy of the daily press throughout the country. They found it was only necessary to purchase the control of 25 of the greatest papers. The 25 papers were agreed upon, emissaries were sent to purchase the policy, national and international of these papers, an agreement was reached, the policy of the papers was bought, to he paid for by the month, an editor was furnished for each paper to properly supervise and edit information regarding the questions of preparedness, militarism, financial policies and other things of national and international nature considered vital to the interests of the purchasers.

This contract is in existence at the present time and it accounts for the news columns of the daily press of the country being filled with all sorts of preparedness arguments and misrepresentations as to the present condition of the United States Army and Navy and the possibility and probability of the United States being attacked by foreign foes.

This policy also included the suppression of everything in opposition to the wishes of the interests served The effectiveness of this scheme has been conclusively demonstrated by the character of stuff carried in the daily press throughout the country since March 1915.

They have resorted to anything necessary to commercialize public sentiment and sandbag the National Congress into making extravagant and wasteful appropriations for the Army and Navy under the false pretense that it was necessary. Their stock argument is that it is for patriotism."

A U.S. Senate committee chaired by Senator Frank Church of Idaho (the Church Committee) in 1976 published its final report the "*Select Committee to Study Governmental Operations with Respect to Intelligence Activities*" concluded:

"Domestic intelligence activity has threatened and undermined the Constitutional rights of Americans to free speech, association and privacy. It has done so primarily because the

Constitutional system for checking abuse of power has not been applied."

"The CIA currently maintains a network of several hundred foreign individuals around the world who provide intelligence for the CIA and at times attempt to influence opinion through the use of covert propaganda. These individuals provide the CIA with direct access to a large number of newspapers and periodicals, scores of press services and news agencies, radio and television stations, commercial book publishers, and other foreign media outlets."

Church argued that the cost of misinforming the world cost American taxpayers an estimated $265 million a year. Lying cost taxpayers money. By analyzing CIA documents Church was able to identify over 50 U.S. journalists who were employed directly by the Agency. He was aware that there were a lot more who enjoyed a very close relationship with the CIA who were

"being paid regularly for their services, to those who receive only occasional gifts and reimbursements from the CIA".

Operation Mockingbird was a secret Central Intelligence Agency campaign headed by Allen Dulles to influence domestic and foreign media beginning in the 1950s. In a Rolling Stone article by Carl Bernstein October 1977 called "CIA and the Media" he alleged that one of the most important journalists under the control of Operation Mockingbird was Joseph Alsop, a nephew of Theodore Roosevelt, because of his family ties to the Roosevelt's, Alsop soon became well-connected in Washington, his articles appeared in over 300 different newspapers. Other journalists alleged by *Rolling Stone Magazine* to have been willing to promote the views of the CIA included Stewart Alsop (*New York Herald Tribune*), Ben Bradlee (*Newsweek*), James Reston (*New York Times*), Charles Douglas Jackson (*Time Magazine*), Walter Pincus (*Washington Post*), William C. Baggs (*The Miami News*), Herb Gold (*The Miami News*) and Charles Bartlett (*Chattanooga Times*).

Turning to the broadcast media the radio and television stations were all under the umbrella of NBC, RCA, CBS and ABC. The founder of RCA Globalist **Owen D. Young** was a CFR Director from 1927 to 1940 as GE's president and chairman he helped found NBC and as a Rockefeller associate he was on the board of trustees of the Rockefeller Foundation. Under the tutelage of Owen Young David Sarnoff became President of NBC and RCA a position he held until 1970. With Young's influence Sarnoff became a member of the Rockefeller Brothers Fund panel to report on U.S. foreign policy. Together Rockefeller and Sarnoff developed the Rockefeller Center as RCA agreed to be its first tenant and together they created what RCA head David Sarnoff dubbed "Radio City."

NBC's rival CBS founder William S. Paley was an army colonel working in US intelligence during World War II, Paley served in the psychological warfare branch in the Office of War Information, under General Dwight Eisenhower. It was while based in London, England; during the war that Paley came to know Edward R. Murrow CBS's head of European news. Paley was a trustee of the Rockefeller Foundation from the 1930's and became its president in 1962.

The Federal Communication Commission in May 1940 issued a "Report on Chain Broadcasting." They claimed monopoly anti-trust concerns and forced the sale by RCA of one of its chains. The spinoff became ABC and was purchased by Edward Noble the founder of the Life Saver Company.

With such a concentration of ownership the ability through corporate and financial associations to manipulate the press has been confirmed over history, as we have seen that stories leaked out in the press, have been found to be erroneous when finally investigated for the truth. America Presidents have garnished support for war, time and again on false information leaked to the press by covert agents. Soldiers are sent to die on lies by the press that make the public believe that the reasons for war are justified. As evidenced by the recent war in Iraq (operation Iraqi Freedom) press leaks by CIA reports of Saddam Hussein's Weapons of Mass Destruction became the justification for the military action. The *"U.S. Senate Select Committee on Intelligence: Senate Intelligence Committee Unveils Final Phase II Reports on Prewar Iraq Intelligence"*. The Senate Intelligence Committee found in 2008 that the administration "misrepresented the intelligence and the threat from Iraq". The Iraq war has produced 5875 American casualties. It was started on a lie. It continues to this day and is reminiscing of Vietnam. A war started by the false information received by the press on the Gulf of Tonkin incident.

*"They will **engage their country in ridiculous, expensive, fantastical wars,** to keep the minds of men in continual hurry and agitation, and under constant fears and alarms; and, by such means, deprive them both of leisure and inclination to look into publick miscarriages. Men, on the contrary, will, instead of such inspection, be disposed to fall into all measures offered, seemingly, **for their defence, and <u>will agree to every wild demand</u> made by those who are betraying them.***"

Cato's Letter No. 17
John Trenchard (February 18, 1721)

The people of America must realize that the instrument of their betrayal is the main stream media. This concentration of newspapers, news networks, magazines and web sites are controlled by a government behind our government that perpetually controls public sentiment in their favor. In this world black is white, up is down, in is out and deception is so complete that despotism rides in on white horse waving the American flag while the public attends the ticker tape parade. Politicians are elected to congress riding the wave of public sentiment that has been shaped by the distorted media. Washington doesn't want to protect freedom and liberty. They want to control everything about our lives. They want to grow government until it owns every square inch of America and the media is used to that end. That is why polls are so important to the political process. Polls are used to determine how well the main stream media is doing their job of indoctrinating the public with their guile. The main stream media has a large influence on audiences by their choice of what stories to consider news worthy. The mass media sets the agenda for public opinion by highlighting certain issues. News outlets act as custodians of information and make choices about what to report setting the thought environment of the public. The mass media has the ability to mentally order and organize our world for us by telling us what to think about.

How can the average American find a mentally safe haven in the midst of this pseudo-matrix world? How can the public have a gauge by which to judge what they are being told by the talking heads? How can we know when the basic principles of liberty and freedom are being discarded by the main stream media and replaced by tyranny? What is tyranny? What is freedom? What is liberty? What is America? Who can give us a compass that will navigate us through the current rhetoric? The answer to that question lies in the past. The definitions of liberty, freedom, America and tyranny can be found in the writing of our forefathers. Their knowledge is the only navigational instrument we need to be sure we are not being duped.

Every American needs to study the Declaration of Independence, the Constitution and Bill of rights, the Articles of Confederation, the Federalist papers, the Jefferson letters, George Washington's farewell address, John Locke's Second Treatise of Civil Government, Thomas Paine's Common Sense, Patrick Henry's speech, the Cato letters, John Adams's Thoughts on Government, Adam Smith's The Wealth of Nations and the Fairfax Resolves by George Mason. The biographies of these and other founding fathers of liberty and freedom in America could be used to sturdy your foundation of American truth against the lies and hypocrisy of a government gone mad. The national travesty in education is that these founding documents are not required study in our public schools. It makes you wonder about the control that the federal leviathan has on the minds of our children and what they choose to censure from American thought.

Without a deep rooted education in early American thought the public at large will not be able to disseminate what they here in the media. The mass media wants to turn the people into sheeple. They have an Orwellian philosophy that tries to press all people into a world mold. Free will and free thought is considered an ailment by those who are using our government to steal our liberty and freedom. The American patriot is the last barrier to a global authority.

I'll get you started with Patrick Henry's March 23, 1775 speech in Virginia "Give me Liberty or Give me Death" Given in response to the British occupation before the Revolutionary War.

"No man thinks more highly than I do of the patriotism, as well as abilities, of the very worthy gentlemen who have just addressed the house. But different men often see the same subject in different lights; and, therefore, I hope it will not be thought disrespectful to those gentlemen if, entertaining as I do opinions of a character very opposite to theirs, I shall speak forth my sentiments freely and without reserve. This is no time for ceremony. The question before the house is one of awful moment to this country. For my own part, I consider it as nothing less than a question of freedom or slavery; and in proportion to the magnitude of the subject ought to be the freedom of the debate. It is only in this way that we can hope to arrive at the truth, and fulfill the great responsibility which we hold to God and our country. Should I keep back my opinions at such a time, through fear of giving offense, I should consider myself as guilty of treason towards my country, and of an act of disloyalty toward the Majesty of Heaven, which I revere above all earthly Kings.

Mr. President, it is natural to man to indulge in the illusions of hope. We are apt to shut our eyes against a painful truth, and listen to the song of that siren till she transforms us into beasts. Is this the part of wise men, engaged in a great and arduous struggle for liberty? Are we disposed to be of the numbers of those who, having eyes, see not, and, having ears, hear not, the things which so nearly concern their temporal salvation? For my part, whatever anguish of spirit it may cost, I am willing to know the whole truth, to know the worst, and to provide for it.

I have but one lamp by which my feet are guided, and that is the lamp of experience. I know of no way of judging of the future but by the past. And judging by the past, I wish to know what there has been in the conduct of the British ministry for the last ten years to justify those hopes with which gentlemen have been pleased to solace themselves and the House. Is it that insidious smile with which our petition has been lately received?

Trust it not, sir; it will prove a snare to your feet. Suffer not yourselves to be betrayed with a kiss. Ask yourselves how this gracious reception of our petition comports with those warlike preparations which cover our waters and darken our land. Are fleets and armies necessary to a work of love and reconciliation? Have we shown ourselves so unwilling to be reconciled that force must be called in to win back our love? Let us not deceive ourselves, sir. These are the implements of war and subjugation; the last arguments to which kings resort. I ask gentlemen, sir, what means this martial array, if its purpose be not to force us to submission? Can gentlemen assign any other possible motive for it? Has Great Britain any enemy, in this quarter of the world, to call for all this accumulation of navies and armies? No, sir, she has none. They are meant for us: they can be meant for no other. They are sent over to bind and rivet upon us those chains which the British ministry have been so long forging. And what have we to oppose to them? Shall we try argument? Sir, we have been trying that for the last ten years. Have we anything new to offer upon the subject? Nothing. We have held the subject up in every light of which it is capable; but it has been all in vain. Shall we resort to entreaty and humble supplication? What terms shall we find which have not been already exhausted? Let us not, I beseech you, sir, deceive ourselves. Sir, we have done everything that could be done to avert the storm which is now coming on. We have petitioned; we have remonstrated; we have supplicated; we have prostrated ourselves before the throne, and have implored its interposition to arrest the tyrannical hands of the ministry and Parliament. Our petitions have been slighted; our remonstrance's have produced additional violence and insult; our supplications have been disregarded; and we have been spurned, with contempt, from the foot of the throne! In vain, after these things, may we indulge the fond hope of peace and reconciliation?

There is no longer any room for hope. If we wish to be free--if we mean to preserve inviolate those inestimable privileges for which we have been so long contending--if we mean not basely to abandon the noble struggle in which we have been so long engaged, and which we have pledged ourselves never to abandon until the glorious object of our contest shall be obtained--we must fight! I repeat it, sir, we must fight!

An appeal to arms and to the God of hosts is all that is left us! They tell us, sir that we are weak; unable to cope with so formidable an adversary. But when shall we be stronger? Will it be the next week, or the next year? Will it be when we are totally disarmed, and when a British guard shall be stationed in every house? Shall we gather strength but irresolution and inaction? Shall we acquire the means of effectual resistance by lying supinely on our backs and hugging the delusive phantom of hope, until our enemies shall have bound us hand and foot? Sir, we are not weak if we make a proper use of those means which the God of nature hath placed in our power. The millions of people, armed in the holy cause of liberty, and in such a country as that which we possess, are invincible by any force which our enemy can send against us. Besides, sir, we shall not fight our battles alone. There is a just God who presides over the destinies of nations, and who will raise up friends to fight our battles for us. The battle, sir, is not to the strong alone; it is to the vigilant, the active, the brave. Besides, sir, we have no election. If we were base enough to desire it, it is now too late to retire from the contest. There is no retreat but in submission and slavery! Our chains are forged! Their clanking may be heard on the plains of Boston! The war is inevitable--and let it come! I repeat it, sir, let it come.

It is in vain, sir, to extenuate the matter. Gentlemen may cry, Peace, Peace--but there is no peace. The war is actually begun! The next gale that sweeps from the north will bring to our ears the clash of resounding arms! Our brethren are already in the field! Why stand we here idle? What is it that gentlemen wish? What would they have? Is life so dear, or peace so sweet, as to be purchased at the price of chains and slavery? Forbid it, Almighty God! I know not what course others may take; **but as for me, give me liberty or give me death!**

Chapter 10

"The end of the cold war and the search for a new enemy"

During World War II the United States supplied the Communist Soviet Union with massive military aid. According to US state department documents prepared by the CENTER OF MILITARY HISTORY, UNITED STATES ARMY, WASHINGTON, D. C., 2000 Library of Congress Catalog Card Number 52-60791 First Printed 1952-CMH Pub 8-1, and U.S. Government Printing Office Washington.

FDR passed the lend-lease act after the German attack on the Soviet Union, making the United States an auxiliary of Great Britain in the task of delivering supplies to the USSR through the Persian Corridor. This route, joining Soviet territory to warm water across the mountains and deserts of Iran, was one of five by which 17 1/2 million long tons of supplies were carried from Western Hemisphere ports to Soviet destinations. It is difficult to visualize 17 1/2 million long tons but 2,803 ships crossed the seas to carry them, a fleet morc than nine times as numerous as that which mounted the Anglo-American invasion of North Africa in November 1942. The total tonnage figure nearly matches the 22 million long tons landed on the Continent of Europe for the American forces between January 1942 and May 1945. In committing munitions and equipment to the titanic defense of Stalingrad, the cargos contained 39,645 aircraft, 70,407 combat vehicles, 873,846 trucks, 144,361 tons of guns and ammo, 995,368 tons of food and 1,248,547 tons of metal and metal products, for all this America received no payment.

After the Allies' won the war, the big three FDR, Churchill and Stalin met at what became known as the Yalta Conference to carve up the world like a thanksgiving turkey. By the end of World War II, thanks to the massive US aid, the Soviets occupied Eastern Europe whiles the US and Western allied forces remained in Western Europe. Beginning with Germany, Stalin, Roosevelt and Churchill divided up zones of occupation. With US and British support the Soviet Union laid the foundation for the Eastern Bloc by directly annexing several countries including eastern Poland, Latvia, Estonia, Lithuania, eastern Finland and eastern Romania. The Eastern European territories liberated from the Nazis and occupied by the Soviet armed forces were added to the Eastern Bloc by converting them into satellite states, East Germany, the People's Republic of Poland, the People's Republic of Bulgaria, the People's Republic of Hungary, the Czechoslovak Socialist Republic, the People's Republic of Romania and the People's Republic of Albania. If the communists were such a threat then why did Roosevelt and Churchill hand Stalin such a great big piece of the world pie?

This was not the first sign of western support for the Soviet Union nor would it be the last, through major Wall Street banking interests the Soviets were heavily financed by western capitalism through financial operatives like Jacob Schiff of Kuhn Loeb & Company and Max Warburg director of M. M. Warburg & CO in Hamburg, Germany.

The *New York Journal American* was a newspaper published from 1937 to 1966. The *Journal American* was the product of a merger between two

New York newspapers owned by William Randolph Hearst: The *New York American* and the *New York Evening Journal*, an afternoon paper. Both were published by Hearst from 1895 to 1937. The *Journal American* was an afternoon publication. On February 3, 1949, the *New York Journal-American* stated, "Today it is estimated even by Jacob's grandson, John Schiff, a prominent member of New York Society, that the old man sank about $20,000,000 for the final triumph of Bolshevism in Russia. Other New York banking firms also contributed." That is an amazing newspaper article to say the least. What it is saying is that Wall Street financed the Bolshevik revolution and the murder of the tsar and his ministers while Anastasia cried in vain like the song says.

Jacob Schiff was the director of the National City Bank of New York, the Equitable Life Assurance Society, Wells Fargo and Union Pacific Railroad and later headed, the investment bank Kuhn, Loeb & Company. Jacob Schiff also sold Japanese bonds in the U.S. for the Japanese war against Russia in 1904, for which he was decorated by the emperor of Japan. He was elected a director of Wells Fargo in September 1914 to succeed his brother-in-law, Paul Warburg, who had resigned to become a founder of the Federal Reserve Bank. This association between Jacob Schiff, Paul Warburg and Max Warburg was the source of the Bolsheviks finance.

Referring to a June 15, 1933, *Congressional Record*, "Congressman Louis T. McFadden, chairman of the House Banking Committee, maintained in a speech to his fellow Congressman:

"The Soviet government has been given United States Treasure funds by the Federal Reserve Board and the Federal Reserve Banks acting through the Chase Bank of JP Morgan and the Guaranty Trust Company and other banks in New York City. Open up the books of Amtorg, the trading organization of the Soviet government in New York, and of Gostorg, the general office of the Soviet Trade Organization, and of the State Bank of the Union of Soviet Socialist Republics and you will be staggered to see how much American money has been taken from the United States' Treasury for the benefit of Russia.... Those 12 private credit monopolies were deceitfully and disloyally foisted upon this country by bankers who came here from Europe and who repaid us for our hospitality by undermining our American intuitions. Those bankers took money out of this country to Finance Japan in a war against Russia. They created a reign of terror in Russia with our money in order to help that war along. They instigated the separate peace between Germany and Russia and thus drove a wedge between the allies in the World War. They financed Trotsky's mass meetings of discontent and rebellion in New York. They paid for Trotsky's passage from New York to Russia so that he may assist in the destruction of the Russian Empire. They fomented and instigated the Russian revolution and they placed a large fund of American dollars at Trotsky's disposal in one of their branch banks in Sweden so that through him Russian homes might be thoroughly broken up and Russian children flung far and wide from their natural protectors."

Amtorg Trading Corporation was the first Soviet trade representation in the United States when Armand Hammer established it in New York in 1924 through the amalgamation of the American firms Products Exchange Corporation (1919). Armand Hammer born in Manhattan to Russian-born immigrants Julius and Rose Lipshitz ran Occidental Petroleum. Hammer made a trip to the Soviet Union in 1921 four years after the Bolshevik revolution. Hammer claimed he was the only man in history friendly with both Vladimir Lenin and Ronald Reagan.

Jacob Schiff had close associations with E.H. Harriman whose son W. Averell Harriman another globalist and director of the CFR was a prime supporter of the Soviets with finance and diplomatic assistance and became US Ambassador to the Soviets. The Guaranty Trust, run by Harriman and Morgan had a vice-president by the name of Max May who became the first vice president of the first soviet international bank RUSKOMBANK. As reported by The U.S. State Dept. Decimal File, 861.516/129, August 28, 1922 A State Dept. report from Stockholm, dated October 9, 1922 (861.516/137), U.S. State Dept. Decimal File, 861.516/137, Stockholm, October 9, 1922. The report was signed by Ira N. Morris commissioner-general to Italy (1913) and as U.S. minister to Sweden (1914–23). *"It was based on a syndicate that involved the former Russian private bankers and some new investment from German, Swedish, American, and British bankers. Known as the RUSKOMBANK, it was headed by Olof Aschberg; its board consisted of tsarist private bankers, representatives of German, Swedish, and American banks, and, of course, representatives of the Soviet Union."*

After the Bolsheviks took power, the Rockefeller's Standard Oil of New Jersey bought up Russian oil fields, while Standard Oil of New York built the soviets a refinery and made an arrangement to market their oil in Europe. During the 1920's the

Rockefeller's Chase Bank helped found the American-Russian Chamber of Commerce, and was involved in financing Soviet raw material exports and selling Soviet bonds in the U.S. According to Senator Barry Goldwater, Chase Manhattan built a truck factory in Russia which could also be used to produce armored vehicles such as tanks and even rocket launchers. An article appeared in the *New York Times* on January 16, 1967, Under the headline, "**Eaton Joins Rockefellers To Spur Trade With Reds**," the article stated:

"An alliance of family fortunes linking Wall Street and the Midwest is going to try to build economic bridges between the free world and Communist Europe. The International Basic- Economy Corporation, controlled by the Rockefeller brothers, and Tower International, Inc., headed by Cyrus S. Eaton, Jr., Cleveland financier, plan to cooperate in promoting trade between the Iron Curtain countries, including the Soviet Union."

Professor Antony C. Sutton studied at the universities of London, Goettingen and California and received his D.Sc. degree from University of Southampton, England. He was an economics professor at California State University Los Angeles and a research fellow at Stanford University's Hoover Institution. During his time at the Hoover Institute he wrote the major study *Western Technology and Soviet Economic Development* (in three volumes), revealing that the United States developed the Soviet Union from its very beginning. Sutton writes in his commentary that the Soviet Union's technology and factories were being provided by the United States corporations funded by US taxpayers while we were fighting in

Vietnam. An auto factory subsidiary of the Ford Motor Company GAZ in the Soviet Union along with steel plants, located in eastern Russia built with the help or technical assistance of U.S. corporations. The volume exposes that the Soviet MIRV enabled missiles could not have been produced without technology, machinery and equipment from US sources.

Not only was the Soviet Union financed by the United States for their conventional artillery but also their nuclear arsenal was created with help from American Scientists. Thanks to communist physicists like Klaus Fuchs who was a German theoretical physicist, working on the Manhattan Project. In 1950 he was convicted of supplying information from the American atomic bomb research to the USSR throughout his career.

The surreal revelation of the truth behind the Cold War takes a long time to absorb into the human consciousness. It is almost like the snooze button on the alarm clock it has to ring true many times before the mind begins to rise out of its slumber of a lifetime of media stupor. As the story begins to unfold with investigation of congressional committees, corporate reports, bank finance reports, corporate directors and their associations, and US trade and commerce reports the darkness of corporate greed comes to stare you right in the eyeballs. The absolute blackout of all information that would have prevented the deception of the last century reveals the complete control of the mass media. Look past what the media says and read between the lines. What has been reported on the surface reveals half the world was divided at Yalta between the communists and the capitalists (that's in the history books), every conflict after that was divided again, Korea was divided into north and south, Vietnam was divided into north and south, one communist regime takes over a country and ten years later it is turned back into some form of democratic socialism or vice versa. Why? A comprehensive view of the surface facts show war makes money, it promotes industry, it forces governments to borrow in excess from their central banks who are more than willingly to create money out of nothing and then profit from the interest paid by the tax payers. Creation of the cold war gave the power brokers the ability to stage war on foreign land to gather the profit of the military industrial complex one show after another. As the curtain closes on one conflict another curtain raises on the next conflict in a perpetual depleting and stockpiling of the instruments of war. Peace cannot be attained as long as the organizing principle of society is for war.

From the oligarchy's warped point of view; war brings enormous profit into the central banks; it relieves the problem of overpopulation; it gives them the ability to confiscate the natural resources of the land where it is fought for the corporate coffers; it makes it possible for them to insert whatever system of government is deemed most advantageous at the time and most importantly it gives them a reason to establish a world government that they can ultimately control. For over 60 years the struggle between capitalism and communism raged on, but somehow, in 1989 it all went away. The movement that started in 1917 with the Bolshevik revolution and to stay in power, caused the death of one hundred million people, took the sign off the door and put up a new one. What happened to all the perpetrators? Basically, nothing. Communist parties in the former communist's states were not outlawed and their members were not brought to justice. Most members of the communist secret police became decision makers in their new governments. Vladimir Putin the president of Russia was head of the KGB. It wasn't as though they could arrest communists in countries where all the people were raised as communists.

In 1989 George Herbert Walker Bush met with Soviet General Secretary Mikhail Gorbachev in a conference on the Mediterranean island of Malta. In a press conference about the meeting Gorbachev responded to reporters, "*I assured the President of the United States that the Soviet Union would never start a hot war against the United States of America. And we would like our relations to develop in such a way that they would open greater possibilities for cooperation.... This is just the beginning. We are just at the very beginning of our road, long road to a long-lasting, peaceful period*". Gorbachev and Bush declared a US-Russian strategic partnership, marking the end of the cold war.

The cold war had reached its effectiveness as a global unification tool. It was intended to create the fear of total nuclear world war and would be counteracted by governments to join forces giving organizations like the United Nations more clout. The only drawback was that it was actually counterproductive because its basic principle was a struggle between nations. Some nation would always have to be left out as the antagonist for it to be effective, hence leaving that nation out of the global unification. A far more effective conflict would have to be developed by the globalists to bring about the consent of the people. People in general are not going to give up their nationalist beliefs and vote to give up their nation's sovereignty without the fear of some conflict looming over the whole world. These conflicts could no longer be struggles between nations they must be struggles against common enemies of all nations of the earth that would create the natural combined sentiments of the nations to combat them as one.

Chapter 11
"The New Global Conflicts"

Myth – Only world government can fix world problems.

"The common enemy of humanity is man.
In searching for a new enemy to unite us, we came up
with the idea that pollution, the threat of global
warming,
water shortages, famine and the like would fit the bill.
All these dangers are caused by human intervention,
and it is only through changed attitudes and behaviour
that they can be overcome. The real enemy then, is
humanity itself."
1993 The First Global Revolution - Club of Rome

The Club of Rome was founded by Aurelio Peccei an Italian scholar and industrialist who worked for the FIAT Auto group in Latin America. He later became president of Oliveri. Peccei founded a consulting firm called Italconsult of which he became chairman. He also got involved with ADELA, a Latin American group of financiers interested in bringing economic growth to Latin America. Peccei gave a speech about the environment at the group's first meeting in 1965. Peccei's speech was read later by the vice-chairman of the State Committee on Science and Technology of the Soviet Union which invited Peccei to Moscow. The vice-chairman later introduced him to Alexander King. Together Peccei and King organized a meeting of economists and scientists to discuss the global problems facing mankind and the importance of working together in a global capacity. At this meeting they decided to call themselves the Club of Rome. They outlined three distinct concepts: 1) a global perspective 2.) The long term 3.) A cluster of intertwined problems they called "the problematique".

Simultaneously a study by Jay Forrester at MIT, on the problems of continued growth on population increase, agriculture production, non-renewable resource depletion, industrial output, and pollution generation was underway. A group of Club of Rome members visited Forrester at MIT and were convinced that his study could be made to work for the global initiative of the Club. In 1971 the findings were published as the Club of Rome's first published work the "Limits to Growth."

The *"Limits to Growth"* is considered to be the most successful environmental publication ever produced and propelled the Club of Rome to its current position of an environmental thought-leader and a major consultant to the United Nations. *"Limits to Growth"* has been translated into more than forty languages and sold more than 30 million copies. Throughout the 1970s and 80s the concept that humanity was irreparably damaging the earth gained popularity and facilitated the formation of mainstream and activist environmental groups.

Not to be outdone, in 1991, only 2 years after the end of the Cold War, the Trilateral Commission came out with its own book *Beyond Interdependence: the Meshing of the World's Economy and the Earth's Ecology*, by Jim MacNeil. Globalist David Rockefeller the founder of the Tri-Lateral Commission and President of the CFR wrote the foreword to the book. Rockefeller states:

"In part this is a physical point. As MacNiell and his co-authors vividly demonstrate, human activities have become so huge that in many instances they are of the same scale as fundamental natural processes. Critical global thresholds are being approached, and perhaps passed. And yet this is not the old argument of Limits to growth—a document that the first director of the Tri-Lateral Commission, Zbigniew Brzezinski, once termed a "pessimist manifesto." The authors instead stress the "growth of limits" evident in the material poverty of much of human kind, the only reasonable alternative is **"sustainable development"**—*a concept that Jim Macneill did so much to advance as Secretary General of the World Commission on environment and development (Brundtland Commission) in its landmark 1987 report Our Common Future."*

The Forward of the book was written by globalist Maurice Strong a Canadian entrepreneur and former under-secretary general of the United Nations.

Strong said this:

"This interlocking...is the new reality of the century, with profound implications for the shape of our institutions of governance, national and international. By the year 2012, these changes must be fully integrated into our economic and political life."

Strong also stated in the opening session of the Rio Conference (Earth Summit II) in 1992 that industrialized countries have:

"Developed and benefited from the unsustainable patterns of production and consumption which have

produced our present dilemma. It is clear that current lifestyles and consumption patterns of the affluent middle class—involving high meat intake, consumption of large amounts of frozen and convenience foods, use of fossil fuels, appliances, home and work-place air-conditioning, and suburban housing—are not sustainable. A shift is necessary toward lifestyles less geared to environmentally damaging consumption patterns."

The Club of Rome and the Tri-Lateral Commission were the catalyst and financiers of many other environmental and sustainability subgroups such as:

The **Club of Madrid** which promotes political change in response to the global sustainability initiatives. The members of the club are former presidents and prime-ministers who have the ability to sway public sentiment. Members include Bill Clinton, Mikhail Gorbachev, Jimmy Carter, Kofi Annan and Helmut Kohl.

The **Gorbachev Foundation of North America (GFNA)**, core mission of the GFNA is to contribute to the strengthening and spread economic liberalization through a program of advocacy, research, and education. GFNA assembles the world's most innovative experts to clarify the myriad of issues which all nations confront, and to develop sustainable political policies.

Green Cross International – also founded by Mikhail Gorbachev has a mission to respond to the combined challenges of security, poverty and environmental degradation to ensure a sustainable and secure future.

To achieve this, GCI: Promotes legal, ethical and behavioural norms that ensure basic changes in the values, actions and attitudes of government, the private sector and civil society, necessary to a sustainable global community.

The United Nations is the foremost promoter of sustainable development. In 1992 the United Nations Conference on Environment and Development (UNCED) with the work of the Club of Rome, and the Tri-Lateral Commission the UN held the Earth Summit II in Rio de Janiero, Brazil. It was at this conference that the UN adopted a plan of action called **Agenda 21**, a 21st century blueprint for action to be taken globally, nationally and locally. Agenda 21 has 40 chapters and is broken down into four sections.

1. Social and Economic Dimensions
2. Conservation and Management of Resources for Development
3. Strengthening the Role of Major Groups
4. Means of Implementation

The Preamble to Agenda 21 states:

"Humanity stands at a defining moment in history. We are confronted with a perpetuation of disparities between and within nations, a worsening of poverty, hunger, ill health and illiteracy, and the continuing deterioration of the ecosystems on which we depend for our well-being. However, integration of environment and development concerns and greater attention to them will lead to the fulfillment of basic needs, improved living standards for all, better protected and managed ecosystems and a safer, more prosperous

future. No nation can achieve this on its' own; but together we can - in a global partnership for sustainable development"

So who is the new enemy of the state? Anyone opposing sustainable development will eventually become an enemy to the world. The global agenda promises to address and contend with economic and environmental issues. These issues that are supposedly intertwined and will form an environmental fascist global society that promotes no war, no poverty, no pollution, no struggles, equally distributing the bounties of the earth to all mankind. Wake up and smell what they are shoveling, to achieve this utopian system of governance, there must be a ruling aristocracy and a massive police presence to enforce its initiative. They will prey on the unsuspecting public to decide the quantity of natural resources that may be used without endangering biodiversity and how much greenhouse gas may be emitted without endangering the global climate. To eliminate war this entity must have the power to disarm all nations, the power to control the population, the power to control all land and it uses, health care, housing and jobs for everyone. Golf courses will be considered a hazard to the environment along with the suburban back yard. These properties will become wetlands for sustainability.

Agenda 21 will usher in the end of national sovereignty (national constitutions will have to take a back seat to sustainability, after all they will propagate "what good would national sovereignty do us if the planet and all life on it is destroyed"), the abolition of private property (already happening in the US with the recent increase in foreclosures), the restructure of the family unit (for population control) and limitations and restrictions on mobility and individual opportunity. Government regulation of what you eat, smoke, play and where you are allowed to live. There is nothing new about this system of governance except the modern names used to describe it. Government control of every single aspect of human life all under the guise of ecology and survival of the human species is fascism, communism and socialism wrapped in a new world rescuing package. The Marxist "politburo" will be replaced with "UNCED", "Redistribution of wealth" will be repackaged as "economic disparity", "soviet expansionism" will be repackaged as "global partnership", "martial law" will be repackaged as "domestic policies" and "WMD's" will not be as threatening as "endangered biodiversity". Alarming to note is that one of its most avid supports is the absolute Marxist and former General Secretary of the Communist Party of the Soviet Union from 1985 until 1991 Mikhail Gorbachev.

The United Nations is power grabbing to regulate every aspect of every life by "falsely indoctrinating" people about the so called benefits of "sustainable development" and the pitfalls of poverty, global warming, population explosion and terrorism. What they don't tell you is that to reach their goals, America and every other country in the world must submit to the doctrine they have premeditated for our consumption.

Where is all the funding coming for this? According to the Worldwide Institute annual reports, "the Rockefeller Brothers Fund and the Winthrop Rockefeller Trust provide core funding for the *State of the World* series. "The *State of the World* report was widely cited as authority for predictions of impending planetary doom by those attending the Earth Summit.

Many examples of the extensive funding of the environmental "movement" by global Establishment foundations can be found, these include: Ford Foundation grants to the Environmental Defense Fund, Friends of the Earth, Natural Resources Defense Council and the World Resources Institute; MacArthur Foundation grants to the Center for International Environmental Law, the Environmental Defense Fund, the Union of Concerned Scientists, and the World Resources Institute; Mott Foundation funding for the Center for International Environmental Law, the Earth Action Network, Friends of the Earth, and the World Resources Institute; and Rockefeller Brothers Fund grants to the Earth Action Alert Network, the Environmental Defense Fund, Friends of the Earth, the Sierra Club Legal Defense Fund, and the Union of Concerned Scientists.

The UN has always chosen global socialist one-worlders for leaders. The Secretary-General at the UN founding conference was Soviet spy Alger Hiss. He was followed as Secretary-General by Norwegian Socialist Trygve Lie, Swedish Socialist Dag Hammarskjold, and Burmese Marxist U Thant, Austrian former Nazi-fascist Kurt Waldheim, Peruvian Socialist Javier Perez DeCuellar, and Egyptian Socialist Boutros Boutros-Ghali. Each has consistently used the full resources of the UN to promote communist, socialist and fascist causes around the world.

Globalist and CFR member George Frost Kennan was an American ambassador to Soviet Russia and Yugoslavia at the height of the cold war, he was known as "the father of containment" and as a key figure in the emergence of the Cold War. He predicted in 1947:

"The main element of any United States policy toward the Soviet Union must be a long-term, patient but firm and vigilant containment of Russian expansive tendencies... Soviet pressure against the free institutions of the Western world is something that can be contained by the adroit and vigilant application of counterforce at a series of constantly shifting geographical and political points, corresponding to the shifts and maneuvers of Soviet policy, but which cannot be charmed or talked out of existence."

After the fall of the Berlin wall and communism George Kennan was heralded as a wise influence for calling for patient action against the Soviets as far back as 1947. On November 12, 1989 he wrote in the Washington Post a new prediction stating:

"The great enemy is not the Soviet Union but the rapid deterioration of our planet as a supporting structure for civilized life."

To further this agenda another globalist and CFR member Michael Oppenheimer a scientist with the Environmental Defense Fund on March 27, 1990 wrote in the New York Times,

"Global warming, ozone depletion, deforestation and overpopulation are the four horsemen of a looming 21st century apocalypse. As the cold war recedes, the environment is becoming the No. 1 international security concern."

Not surprisingly, honest climate scientists rarely have a deep understanding of the big-picture "politics" driving the "global warming" scare.

An exception was the late Dixy Lee Ray. In her 1993 *Environmental Overkill — Whatever Happened to Common Sense?* the former chairman of the Atomic Energy Commission wrote:

*"More and more it is becoming clear that those who support the so-called 'New World Order' or World Government under the United Nations have adopted global environmentalism as a **basis for the dissolution of independent nations and the international realignment of power**."*

If we allow it, this will be the theft of American Sovereignty and the end of America as we know it.

Chapter 12
"What Now?"

Our individual liberties along with our privacy are being eroded daily by social engineering. The freedoms that were given to the American citizens by our Founding Fathers are threatened by legislators that have thrown in their lot with global corporations. Liberal activist are dismembering our basic human rights by pushing the global agenda of regulation of every aspect of life and redistribution of wealth that is removing all traces of the middle class. Small business is the major deterrent to socialism and it too is under attack by our government by taxation and overregulation. Threatening economic collapse that has been purposely engineered by the world banking system and the Federal Reserve poised to undermine and steal everything the population holds dear.

The checks and balances on our government have been removed and the chains of despotism spoken of by James Madison have been snapped. The monster that is our government is on the loose and we may not be able to contain its power any longer. The bill of rights has been usurped by the Patriot Act, the Military Commissions Act, the Real ID Act, conscription, warrantless surveillance, invasions of financial privacy, the war on terror, the war on drugs, gun control, abuses of habeas corpus, cap and trade, NAFTA, the IRS, the Federal Reserve Act and now the unconstitutional health care bill.

If you look carefully at these issues you will notice that the globalist organizations CFR and the UN never speak out against the abuses of these acts. They are the first to point out the poverty and abuses contained in the third world countries around the world but you never hear them champion the causes of the Constitution or the Bill of Rights in America. That is because they are opposed to American liberties as formed by the Founding Fathers and their agenda is for America to submit to their global fascist ideals of world domination. We have allowed The US government to become nothing more than an international organized crime syndicate and military muscle for the agenda of the UN and Global elite.

American CFR corporate membership multinationals have become the mouth piece for the liberty effacing globalization process. Companies like IBM which promotes a new campaign on globalization saying in all there commercial propaganda "let's build a smarter planet". The DOW chemical company's commercial "the human element" stresses their commitment to environmental issues but then debases humanity by declaring that humans are no more important to the earth than any element on the periodic table. GE's mantra "ecoimagination" has lit their torch for globalization with their dancing elephant.

Why is it that you never see a multinational corporation spending millions of dollars on a campaign to promote liberty in America? The simple reason is it doesn't pay. The only ones who can therefore promote liberty are the American citizens who actually still care that we have any. Those who have been lulled to sleep by the mass media singing their lullaby song of globalization don't realize what they are losing and most of them have been duped into thinking that the global way is a benevolent ideal that will look out for their best interest. The only thing the globalist agenda has in store for the citizens of the world is SERFDOM. That's right SERFDOM! They rule and you work for their benefit this is their final solution. You keep swallowing the Kool-Aid that is being poured down your throat by the UN, CFR, Tri-Lateral Commission, NBC, CBS, ABC, FOX, Associated Press, Rueters, GE, IBM, Wall Street, the board of governors of the Federal Reserve open market committee and the unscrupulous politicians that have made their way into the halls of congress by lying to voters and the only liberty you will have left is the liberty to work for slave labor rates.

"When the people fear their government, there is tyranny; when the government fears the people, there is liberty." Thomas Jefferson

The tyranny that was faced by our Founding Fathers has raised its ugly head again and is boldly challenging those who love liberty and patriotism. It's time to rise up in a grass roots effort to eradicate the evil ideology undermining American sovereignty and hold the perpetrators accountable to what it is "treason". We must find brave men and women who are running for political offices in all of our communities that will commit to rolling back the government to an era of constitutionalism bringing back the rights of the people. The time for apathy is gone the time for action is long overdue the campaign for liberty is mounting and will only succeed if you participate.

Your party affiliation doesn't matter anymore the onslaught against liberty is not a social issue and being a democrat or a republican means nothing to this struggle. The policies of these political parties have always been a diversionary tactic by the globalists to pit the American people against each other on social issues while they are at work stripping our liberties. If we are busy fighting each other we won't have the ability to turn our efforts and fight together for our liberties. The infractions of the past that have torn the fabric of freedom came by democrats as well as republicans. No matter which party has controlled the government the deficit rose. Neither party has turned back inflation nor have they stopped the warfare state.

The problem of the people is they simply don't care to or don't have the time to educate themselves on the current liberty killing politics of today. They get home from work, have diner and turn on their local news. Few people question what they're told or why things are presented in a certain way by the mass media. We need to look past our differences, read between the lines and unite in a common cause to bring back the principles of freedom. There are very important social issues faced by our nation at this time but some of these issues must be tabled temporarily to make room for basic reparations to the Constitution and Bill of Rights.

The following are some of the challenges facing America today that if they are not properly met will capitulate our way of life and may even lead to World War III.

- America needs to adopt a non interventionist foreign policy. Bring our troops home from abroad immediately and begin a dialogue of real peace and stability. We must stop being the military muscle for UN Policy. The war on terror has been created by our very own foreign policy guided by the corrupt CFR. America has throughout history made huge interventions into countries to prop up regimes for the purpose of stealing the natural resources of the indigenous people for the benefit of multinational corporations. If a foreign country were to come to the United States for the express purpose of stealing our natural resources we would nuke them off the planet but when the United States does it we call it foreign aid. We have hundreds of military bases on foreign soil it is time to close them down, they are the drain on our economy. Our military should only be used to protect our borders and our liberties just like General Smedely Butler said.

- Liquidate the Federal Reserve and use their assets to pay off the deficit and whatever is left over give back to the taxpayer. Then commit to the free market system that builds the middle class and makes it possible for the citizens of America to chase the American dream. Institute a treasury system of sound money by the government that gives the creation of monetary policy back to the people of the United States and away from the private bankers. Amend the Constitution to keep our country from ever submitting our sovereignty to outside private financial interests.

- Amend the Constitution to never let the sovereign power of the United States be undermined by global supranational organizations like the UN or any other system that doesn't possess elected officials by the people of the United States.

- Prosecute the CFR as the criminal organization that it is along with the Tri-Lateral Commission, the Brooking Institute and the Open Society Institute. Liquidate the assets of these organizations.

- Repeal the Sixteenth Amendment and produce a fair tax that is apportioned by the several states as was the original intent of the founders.
- Repeal the Seventeenth Amendment and give the states back their right to appoint the Senators out of the state legislators and make laws that would abolish corporate lobbies in the halls of Congress.
- Redefine the "commerce clause" as to not let the government use it to destroy our liberties.
- Reinstate a commitment to the Tenth Amendment giving back to state and local government all powers that are not expressly defined in the "enumerated powers of the Federal Government". Allow the State and local government to be the political laboratories for passing legislation for social issues that divide us so they could foster a competition to produce the best laws for the people.
- Amend the Constitution to include provisions for a mandatory balanced fiscal budget for the operation of the Federal Government.
- Abolish the Department of Education. The federal government has never educated one child it is not constitutional for them to do it or interfere in matters that should be reserved for the local community. The very idea that a group of legislators and bureaucrats in D.C. can design a curriculum capable of meeting the needs of every American schoolchild is ridiculous.
- Abolish the department of energy which would be unconstitutional without the perversion of the commerce clause.

- Abolish the Patriot Act it is in direct opposition to the 4th amendment and therefore makes it unconstitutional.
- Repeal Obama Care it has already been ruled unconstitutional.
- Close our borders and repeal NAFTA raise tariffs on all products that are produced by low paid foreign labor. The price of products from overseas should be equal to the price of products if they were produced in American factories. This is the only thing that will bring manufacturing back to America and create real jobs again.
- Limit the size of federal legislation so it can be read by our lawmakers. 2000 page bills are not conducive to an organized system of administration that could be understood by everyone.

These are the issues that are directly related to American freedom. These are the loop holes where global corporatism makes its way into your life through the government. The only thing between you and SERFDOM is the chains on the government tied to the Constitution. The Bill of Rights is the ball and chain shackled to the leg of Washington. Let us reinforce these chains with sound governing principles and honorable men and women that understand the instruments that are used against liberty and freedom. Our children must be educated to know the true history of America not the rewritten lies that are supported by an educational system that refuses to record the truth. Lies that don't even know they are lies because they are the grandchildren and great grandchildren of lies. For if future generations are not prepared for the onslaught of despotism they will end up in the exact same predicament we are currently experiencing.

The government of the bankers, by the lawyers and for the corporations must be brought back to the government of the people, by the people and for the people. We can only do this with the participation of every single person that wants to preserve the freedom of America. Get to work connecting with people in your community that stand for freedom. Use the internet to find people in your area that can help organize and volunteer, join others that have already started. Sign up for liberty movements and forums to learn the basic principles of freedom. The fires of liberty have been lit and are burning across America young as well old must join the movement. Don't wait do it today tomorrow is too late. The enemy never sleeps, they have their agenda it is to steal your liberty and freedom, they have been at for a long time and they are not going to quit. The war is on and there is no escaping it, don't let the think tanks roll over you while you sleep, wake up now and join the program.

www.ingramcontent.com/pod-product-compliance
Lightning Source LLC
Chambersburg PA
CBHW072119270326
41931CB00010B/1602